The *Editor's* Page

Edited by GUSTAVE L. WEINSS

Springtime's Coming

To those of us who live in the north temperate zone—and especially if Old Winter has been generous with his cold weather and snowstorms—there is nothing more inviting than the return of springtime.

And springtime's surely coming. In fact, it's already here.

Haven't you noticed how the days are lengthening? And haven't you breathed the delightful, balmy, fragrant air?

With the migrating birds returning and Mother Nature putting on her splendor, hasn't your pulse been quickening? Aren't you being filled with new inspiration and hope?

We all should be affected in this way, to say the least. Indeed, we would be very unappreciative if springtime with her glorious changes did not arouse in us the spirit of being up and doing, of getting at our work with new zest and vim.

I, for one, am glad to see spring, and I'm sure there are many more who are glad with me.

□

Those Who Win

An acquaintance of mine said to me one day, "Do you know it just seems that I can't win out; always something seems to be against me."

But as I looked into his record, I was not surprised, for he did not seem to comprehend the qualifications of those who win. His greatest drawback was himself. Just because he wants certain things, he seems to think he must have them. But he lacks the gumption to work for them.

Those who win are those who work and keep on trying. They are just average persons like you and me, or, as Charles Bartlett says, they are "not built on any particular plan nor blessed with any peculiar luck; they are just steady and earnest and full of pluck."

"Be the Best of Whatever You Are"

If you can't be a pine on the top of the hill,
  Be a scrub in the valley—but be
The best little scrub at the side of the rill;
  Be a bush if you can't be a tree.

If you can't be a bush, be a bit of the grass,
  Some highway to happier make,
If you can't be a muskie, then just be a bass—
  But the liveliest bass in the lake!

We can't all be captains, we've got to be crew,
  There's something for all of us here;
There's big work to do and there's lesser to do,
  And the task we must do is the near.

If you can't be a highway, then just be a trail,
  If you can't be the sun, be a star;
It isn't by size that you win or you fail—
  Be the best of whatever you are.

But those who win must work for their success. That is the secret. They dare not shirk trouble nor labor, but must use their head and hands, and, above all, try again and again.

So, you see, no person has a monopoly on the ability to be successful. This is as free as the air we breathe, and you and I can enjoy it just as well as any one else. In fact, we can all be classed among those who win *if* we turn our wishes into actions, our desires into deeds.

□

Great Deeds or Good Ones?

If you had your choice, which would you prefer, an opportunity to perform *great* deeds or one to perform *good* deeds?

If you were to choose the latter instead of the former, you would be making the better choice, for the opportunity to perform a really great deed may never come, whereas every new day renews the opportunity for good deeds.

And, what is more, the doing of many good deeds, while it may not lead to fame, will surely result in much happiness—to yourself and to those who benefit by your works.

□

Be the Best

In a little publication called *Macograms*, I ran across a poem that impressed me so much that I have reproduced it here for your benefit.

No loftier ambition could any one have than to be the best in his or her chosen work. Being the best makes for success, even though it may not mean that you are "the greatest of them all."

Everybody, you know, cannot be an outstanding figure, a great personage, a leader. There must be some who make up the rank and file. Still, there is nothing to hinder any of us from being "the best of whatever we are" if—and there's that *if* again—if we really want to occupy that coveted place.

Advance Fashion Notes—Summer, 1923

IN a general way, the preference of the elegant woman turns toward the straight line, although the draped effect has not been abandoned, especially for evening robes, on account of the distinguished appearance it imparts. Many draped robes will be seen both in the large stores and in the dressmakers' shops.

The skirt remains fairly long, sometimes reaching down to the ankles, except for the tailor-made costumes, where it is a little higher in order to give a sharper outline and to allow for the tightness of the skirt. The waist line has a tendency to be higher, and in some houses it will even resume its normal position, in which case the skirt is cut with more fulness on the sides.

As regards the sleeves, they are sometimes very narrow and long, but generally cut down to a simple "mancheron" (short sleeve) to hide the shoulder, and in some cases even completely done away with, even for walking-out dresses.

THE fashionable colors will include the whole range of shell tones and "vert amande" (almond green) as well as "bleu chine" (a shade a little lighter than king's blue), jade green, and vieux rouge (old red).

Certain printed materials will not require any trimmings.

The single-color materials will be trimmed with cashmere, embroidery, and pearl beads. Much use will be made of a new dull pearl bead and small varicolored cellophane trimmings. These trimmings, which are very original, will, in nearly every case, be of geometric shape.

One of the latest trimmings is formed of "paillettes de drap" (dripping spangles) joined together by gold thread.

Metal embroidery and material worked with gold and silver wire will hold a preeminent position.

Dresses of a uniform color, or shades of the same color, will be abundant. The classical tailor-made, the most simple being always the most "chic," will be either a costume in three pieces—skirt, jacket, and blouse to match, or a complete robe and jacket. Good use will be made of a new, very soft alpaca.

There will also be many dresses consisting of a robe and cape, not only for tailor-mades, but also for soft-material dresses, such as crêpe marocain.

For afternoon wear, mantle robes in reps (twilled silk or wool) will be in vogue.

WOMAN'S INSTITUTE OFFICES
Paris, France

IN the summer, foulard (printed silk) will meet with the same success as last year. For the seaside and the country, the knitted

---

THIS letter came to me from Paris just when Fashion Service went to press. It corresponds so closely with what we have given you there that I believe it will interest you. I want you to have every bit of available information so that your clothes will be more beautiful and more satisfactory than ever before.

In planning clothes for yourself, first read all the authentic fashion news available and observe style drawings, shop windows, and well-dressed women.

Then be honest with yourself and study your type. If you are large, admit it and plan your clothes accordingly. If your skin and hair are hard in texture, these, too, must be admitted so as to be corrected. By this I do not mean that you should be overmodest and unappreciative of your good points. Some women who look very splendid in their clothes belittle their appearance. Always "give credit where credit is due," even when it is about yourself.

If you are small or very large, beware of the large-figured patterns that are shown in such abundance in the shops this season.

If your skin is very fair and you hair soft and good to look at, and you are small or medium large, you can wear the bright, definite colors with good result. Otherwise, avoid them. Work for harmony in color and for becomingness in line, and be ever alert for distinctiveness. There are enough subdued colors, enough soft materials, enough of every kind so that every woman may have something right in every way.

Mary Brooks Picken

---

stuffs, which were so popular last year, will be replaced by Melton cloth (molleton) and printed duvetyn.

With a rather short skirt will be worn a small smoking jacket in plain duvetyn.

We shall see robes of linon, printed and plain muslin, and flowered prints. Even very inexpensive prints are made up distinctively and are very popular.

The principal shades will be red, white, green, and orange; also, tan, gray, and the pastel shades for sheer dresses.

EVENING robes will be long and will often have a train. The materials will be very rich and embroidered heavily with gold and silver. We shall also see black robes embroidered with pearl beads of all colors, as well as pure white robes. Black will be reserved for evening wear.

For the evening, capes will still be preferred and will be made of very rich material. Some are circular in shape, but others, on the contrary, form large sleeves cut in points and falling on both sides. Still others are of straight pieces with fulness folded or held in at the back collar, for wraps are generous in size and linings, soft and lovely.

THERE will be more novelty in the hats than in the dresses. At the beginning of the season, there will be many small hats, especially bell-shaped hats, some with the brim turned up behind. There will be much less simplicity —very light ribbon and aigrette trimmings, very long paradise feathers placed under the brim and falling down over the shoulder. There are also violets of all colors arranged in large "cocardes" giving a very taking effect. Some hats are formed of a ribbon crown, the brim being of straw and turned up at the side or in front. Veils, which are placed half-way up the crown and fall over the sides, are still in favor.

In the summer will be seen large capelines of "crin" (horsehair) or of light straw completely covered with flowers, and prettily draped toques of straw and satin.

The evening head-dress, so as to be in harmony with the richness of the robes, will be formed of a head-band of ribbon with a large feather falling over the shoulder, a ribbon shape worked with gold or silver, a head-band with gold and silver flowers, a strip of black velvet with a bush of feathers springing from behind, or aigrettes, forming a cache-peigne (to cover the back comb).

The little bell shape in Scotch straw will be the most fashionable head-dress for the seaside and country.

Artful Ribbon Effects for *Sports* Wear

By MARY MAHON
Department of Millinery

IN the development of very smart sports models, all the different millinery materials are used, but rarely, if ever, is there a hat finished without the introduction of ribbon in some form or other. Sometimes the entire hat is constructed of ribbon; then again, a jaunty bow or a hand-made garniture in floral effect is applied to a model developed of another fabric.

The freedom of design for sports hats, established by the variety of shapes and the diversity of trimmings and color combinations, recognizes no controlling influence; consequently, all sizes, shapes, and materials are utilized in the development of sports hats, which assume a rather dressy aspect this season.

IN millinery parlance, there are two distinctive kinds of sports hats; the extremely simple type, which is appropriate for those who participate in the games and, while rather plain, is not lacking in artistic design, and the more dressy type, in which those on the side lines are privileged to indulge. Whatever form the sports hat takes, however, its first choice in the matter of trimming falls to ribbon. The frilled scroll, the motif, and the decorative cocarde are the most popular expressions, as evidenced by the models illustrated on this page.

THOUGH classed as a sports hat, the model at the top is pretentious enough as to type and has such unusual ornamentation that it would easily serve as a smart afternoon hat. The foundation is a medium-size poke frame. Changeable taffeta, "mimosa to rose," is used to cover the upper brim plain and make the regulation balloon crown. A tagal plateau is used for the under facing, the edge being finished with a binding of metal ribbon. In an all-over scroll design, three shades of frilled metal ribbon wind colorful paths about the crown and top brim, after which it is interspersed with tiny tuscan buttons, or varicolored glass beads may be substituted. The ribbon and the buttons are applied to the crown before it is attached to the brim.

THE model illustrated at the left can be made wearable with several different colored sweaters or sports coats by using ribbon in three different colors for the motifs. The bell-shaped crown and the under facing of the brim are made of white visca braid, and the top facing is fitted with silk-warp crêpe.

In applying the braid to the under facing, allow the first, or outer, row to extend its full width beyond the edge; then, after the top facing is applied, turn this braid over the edge to form a binding. The diamond-shaped motifs, made of frilled ribbon in three different colors, are applied to the crown in diadem effect. Straw buttons, or varicolored beads, are used to outline the motifs on this model also.

THE rarest and most valuable kind of taste is that which suggests new and novel things without featuring the extreme, as the model at the right evidences. A decidedly new novelty ribbon is selected for developing

the hat; it relies, however, on the simple, but ever becoming, chin-chin for outline in frame.

This flexible brim is made over a wire mold according to the method described in Art. 34, *Special-Purpose Millinery*. In this case, the ribbon, being narrower, can be sewed spirally on the brim instead of being cut at the end of each row in the back. Also, in attaching the first row of ribbon around the brim, let it extend its full width beyond the edge. Before the brim is removed from the mold, hem a row of brace wire into the portion of the ribbon that extends beyond the edge; then after it is removed from the mold, shape the brim out at each side.

For the crown, sew the ribbon spirally over a mold, and in order to help it retain its shape, use a very thin pressed crown of crinoline under it. Hand-made flowers in two or more shades of novelty ribbon are applied in a flat wreath, overlapping each other around the base of the crown.

FOR any one who takes part in the sports, what could be more appropriate than a soft, medium-size French felt in cork color, the

edge bound in grosgrain ribbon of a deeper tone? The hat shown at the bottom is an exceptionally good model of this type for it is extremely light in weight. It has sufficient brim extension to shade the eyes from the sun's strong rays, and an easy roll on the edge that gives the necessary softness without interfering with the range of vision. This type also permits of several different trimming arrangements, which can be made detachable by means of snaps or hooks and eyes.

The sunburst, or starfish, arrangement shown here is made of No. 100 belting ribbon in two shades of the brown family. To make the ornament, cut seven pieces of ribbon 14 inches long, with the ends cornered, four of the darker shade and three of the lighter. Gather the center of six of the pieces together as for a bow, then twist the extra strip of the darker shade around them and tie firmly for the cross knot. Attach to the side crown and spread the ends of the ribbon in star design, allowing some to tip off the edge.

For variety of trimming, a smart bandanna handkerchief, draped softly around the crown and tied in a loose sailor knot, makes a very successful trimming.

CHARMING straw and felt combinations, also, are especially smart for sports wear. The two-toned effect of straw and felt, in the same or in contrasting colors, produces a depth of coloring and richness of material particularly new and attractive. This type, too, relies principally on ribbon for embellishment, and in all instances the manipulating of ribbon in deft hand touches distinguishes these hats from the ordinary type.

NOT only is ribbon used in the development of sports hats, but its popularity as a garniture for dressy models is unequalled in the history of millinery. For the all-black, transparent dinner hat, heavy black moiré ribbon, satin-faced and about 6 inches wide, is made into graceful flat-looped bows or bunched chow effects. Or it falls in streamers to the shoulders, passes under the chin, and hangs waist length.

Narrow, metal ribbons about $\frac{1}{2}$ inch wide, are laid in loops, one over the other, and all banked solidly to make large cocardes that are sometimes made more colorful by the introduction of brilliant glass beads of every description, which are used as a finish for the center.

Fans of plaited ribbon are used in varied ways. One striking effect is a huge chrysanthemum with thousands of raw-edged petals, all cut from wide ribbon in four or more artfully blended capucine, or tortoise, tones. This, used as a trimming on a dark brown Neapolitan hairbraid dress hat, makes a very striking model.

Plaited and *Wrap-Around* Skirts

By ALWILDA FELLOWS
Department of Dressmaking

THESE new skirts that include a profusion of diminutive plaits are truly fascinating—but would I be safer in selecting a design of the wrap-around tendency? What a wealth of beauty in this shimmering silk—but would a substantial and truly as modish a woolen or a wash fabric serve my purpose better? And these brilliant new colors and gay prints! How enticing they are—

A WIDE range of fabrics is accessible for separate skirts. For service or sports models, camel's hair seems the most popular and novel woolen, although kasha, checked velour, basket weaves, and éponge are also prominent. White skirts in woolens as well

A BORDERED silk, having cork as its principal color and darker tones of cork enlivened by touches of bright color in the border design, seems an ideal fabric for the box-plaited model. Box plaits as wide as this are not at all tedious to baste and press by hand, but, of course, to have the material steam-plaited simplifies the making.

Gray and blue in a heavy novelty silk

but would I do better to hold to plain dark colors or to tan or gray, which are at present evidencing so much smartness even though they are conservative by nature?"

Such are the thoughts that invade one's shopping trips and should receive attention when a new skirt is being planned or purchased. A skirt that is to serve many purposes and is to be worn with a variety of blouses or sweaters must, of necessity, be of a design, fabric, and trimming that will harmonize with each. But if your clothes allowance permits more than one separate skirt, do let your fancy and desire sway you in the selection of at least one model, for besides adding variety to your wardrobe, it will give delightful service, provided it is selected from the viewpoint of becomingness.

IN regard to skirt designs, plaited and wrap-around effects seem to monopolize Fashion's offerings. But what variety there is in plaited models, a great many of them fashioned in the very tiniest of box or side plaits or a combination of both or in various novelty plaitings that have been introduced recently.

In the heavier materials, wider plaits are dominant, although finely plaited effects are shown even in light-weight woolens.

Wrap-arounds are not restricted to any particular kind of material, as they lend themselves as well to sturdy wash fabrics, heavy silks, and woolens as to the very softest of silks, the wrap-around usually being draped in this last instance.

as silks hold much promise, flannel, serge, and broadcloth generally being used for them. In brilliant colors, also, flannels are found in great numbers.

A bewildering array of silks in the loveliest of prints and novelty weaves forecast their acceptance for dressier sports models and separate skirts for more formal wear. Then, too, linen and cotton skirtings in plain and novelty weaves will receive attention later.

A SIMULATED wrap-around that is suitable for a wash fabric, a heavy silk, or a woolen is shown at the extreme left in the group of skirts illustrated on this page. This is of straight cut and may be made lengthwise of the fabric with center-side seams and another seam at the side front, or if the material will permit development on the crosswise grain, merely the side-front seam will be necessary. The trimming may be of hand embroidery in a border design, or it may be of a strip of bordered fabric. On a white flannel skirt, green, orange, or bright-blue yarn embroidery would be very effective.

The next skirt is a typical wrap-around style of printed Roshanara crêpe in which Titian color predominates—a very attractive model to wear with blouses of plain color.

In developing a true wrap-around skirt, let the left front extend from 10 to 18 inches under the right front; then finish the edge of the overlapping right front separately, thus giving ample freedom even in a skirt of narrow effect.

makes up the plaid model, which is another wrap-around style, but this time with the left front overlapping the right and this edge finished very inconspicuously. Simulated bound button-holes placed diagonally and finished with large novelty buttons provide a decorative detail.

This design suggests development, also, in novelty cotton skirtings or plaid or striped woolens.

AN interesting treatment of orange-and-brown checked velour is evident in the next model, in which the straight simple cut of the skirt is modified by an inset of the material at the left side and the belt and pocket trimming are of bias cut for effective contrast.

If a skirt is desired for truly dress-up, or more formal, occasions, a draped model seems the most desirable type. And if this is of navy or black crêpe-satin, it will undoubtedly set off one's very loveliest blouses in a most engaging manner.

The simple draped model that is illustrated is but another version of the wrap-around type attached to a camisole foundation, which prevents a "set" appearance at the waist line. McCall pattern 3144 includes the camisole and skirt portion for a style similar to this.

April Showers for Spring Brides

By LAURA MacFARLANE
Department of Cookery

SURELY there is no lovelier time of the year than April, for fickle though it is, it ushers in brightness after the storms and drab days of the long winter, some of which often linger away into March. Yes, it is the season when

> Every tear is answered by a blossom,
> Every sigh with songs and laughter blent,
> Apple-blooms upon the breezes toss them,
> April knows her own and is content.

It's no wonder that the bride-to-be chooses this month so often for the great day of days. And besides being a charming time for her, it is a delightful one for all her friends, each one of whom wants to do her share in sending the prospective bride into the state of matrimony in the happiest sort of way. Probably no month provides so many offerings in the way of suggestions for the many social events that crowd its days to the utmost. And it is not too early to entertain even for the June bride.

THE first thought that comes to one when a shower is mentioned is, of course, a means to combat it—the parasol. 'Tis true that this idea has been much overworked at such events, but it is ever appropriate and may be used in various new and original ways.

One girl, who gave a linen shower not long ago, procured a large Japanese parasol and covered and decorated it with pink crêpe paper and then attached it in inverted fashion under the dining room chandelier directly over the center of her table. Crêpe-paper apple-blossoms added a dainty touch to the parasol and ended each of the ribbon streamers that were attached to the ribs and ran to the guests' places. The wrapped gifts had been placed in the parasol and when the luncheon dishes were removed from the table, the guests pulled the streamers simultaneously and the parasol turned inside out—a handy trick of the Japanese sort—and a literal shower deluged the bride.

If the gifts are of a kind that are too heavy for a hanging parasol, it may be used as a centerpiece for the table, with streamers running from the edge or the handle, a large ribbon or crêpe-paper bow being used to decorate the handle. For such a parasol, it is well to make a wire frame and then you can have the size you want. Then, again, the parasol idea may be carried out by means of tiny, celluloid parasols, which may be purchased for a small sum at the novelty shops. These may be hung from the chandelier or dome over the table, or used upturned as receptacles for bonbons or nuts.

WHILE the rainbow does not always follow the shower, it is the accompaniment that always brings delight, so why not use the idea in the shower you are going to give this month? You might make a bow out of wire and then cover it with tissue-paper fringe in the seven rainbow colors. This suspended from the lighting fixture over the

Afternoon Showers
Nut-Bread Sandwiches
Ribbon Sandwiches
Mushroom Sandwiches
Fancy Cakes   Nuts
Bonbons
Tea   Hot Chocolate
* * *
Chicken Salad
Mushrooms and Peas
in Patties
Rolls   Olives
French Vanilla Ice Cream
Angel Food
Brownies   Nuts   Coffee

Luncheon Shower
Fruit Cocktail
Creamed Chicken
in Rosettes
Rice Croquettes
Vegetable Salad
Olives   Rolls   Jelly
Maple Parfait
Small Cakes
Coffee   Bonbons   Nuts

Evening Shower
Crab-Flake Cutlets
Cucumber-and-Pineapple Salad
Rolls   Cream Cheese
Fruit Preserves
Strawberry Mousse
Sunshine Cake
Nuts   Bonbons   Coffee

center of the table makes a vantage point for streamers that run to each guest's place, where they are attached to a tiny black pot containing bonbons wrapped in gilt paper. "At the foot of the rainbow lies the pot of gold" you know.

If the rainbow does not actually follow the shower in your arrangement, the gifts, each wrapped in gilt paper, may be brought to the bride in a black pot similar to those used as favors but large enough to hold all of the packages. Or, the pot may be hidden, and rainbow-color streamers may lead her to it.

USUALLY, you will have no trouble planning your decorations if you carry out an idea that signifies the nature of the wedding trip or the life that the honor guest is entering. For instance, for a bride whose wedding journey was to end in a camping trip, one girl planned a camping scene for her table decoration, using a mirror for the lake and arranging in and about it small canoes, boats, houses, and animals, purchased from the toy and novelty shops. For a girl who is to live in the country, a garden scene, with toy rakes, hoes, spades, etc., could be used and tiny wheelbarrows filled with candies chosen for favors.

If the bride-to-be is going to take a long trip to her future home, the shower must of necessity be such as to take little space in her baggage, for undoubtedly this will be a problem that she will have to overcome as much as possible. Then, the shower might

consist of handkerchiefs, articles to be used in traveling, a series of steamer letters, silk stockings, or other necessities that will take little space. Whatever is chosen may be concealed in a tiny trunk or small suit case or traveling bag used as a center decoration.

MUCH fun can be had at kitchen showers, for the articles may be dressed in all sorts of freakish ways to represent animals, toy dolls, etc., and presented unwrapped, or they may be disguised with their wrappings and the recipient then asked to guess their contents before she opens them. You will be surprised to find out how many original ideas can be brought out in such wrappings. Another plan is to hang them from a broom handle and present the broom to the bride or they may be piled in a clothes basket, a garbage can, a dish pan, or a coal scuttle.

One girl, who wanted to have a flower luncheon, asked her guests to bring their gifts wrapped or disguised as flowers. Old-fashioned bouquets, roses, tulips, calla lilies, morning glories, chrysanthemums, made a veritable flower garden for the center of her table, some of the wrappings being made out of paper and others out of handkerchiefs, wash cloths, and towels.

Then, she employed the flower idea throughout her menu, cutting her sandwiches to represent four-leaf clovers and her radishes to resemble roses, arranging her salad as a water lily, and serving her ice cream in tiny flower pots covered with crêpe paper and containing real flowers wired and fastened to a toothpick, which was inserted in the center of the filled pot. Ground grape nuts sprinkled over the top of the ice cream gave the appearance of earth. Or, if desired, flower-shape molds of ice cream could be substituted.

SOMETIMES, one wants to give a shower after the wedding. Then, the groom and other men are usually invited. One very clever shower of this kind included a little play. For instance, there was the delightful school-girl age, when some of the guests dressed as little girls romped, jumped rope, and did all such fun-loving things. Later, there was the party age, when the talk was all about dresses and beaus and good times. Then there were the marriage, a home scene, and finally the golden wedding.

After the play, the real bride and groom were yoked together and driven to a room where gifts were piled up in readiness for them. This may be varied and enlarged upon to make it suitable for the honor guests.

Woman's Institute *Question Box*

New Edge Finish

How is the edge of a brim finished when the top is of baronette haircloth and a tagal plateau is used for the under facing?
R. S. M.

If the brim is the same width all around, the edge of the plateau can be turned in the width of one braid and slip-stitched to the top facing, but if the brim is irregular in width, it will require an extra binding. This binding may be made of the same material as the top of the hat or a slick binding of narrow grosgrain ribbon, a popular item this season, may be applied according to the method described in the Instruction Book, *Piece Goods Hats*.

Adding Length to Waist and Skirt

Can you suggest any way of adding length to a dress that is shorter in both the waist and skirt portions than the fashions now being worn?
M. V.

There are a number of ways in which extra length may be provided, but before adopting any one of the following suggestions, consider whether the design of your dress will be marred by the alteration.

If your dress is a blouse style, and you have a piece of self-material from which you may cut a belt 3 or 4 inches wide, separate the waist and skirt portions by inserting the strip of material between them, making the belt in the effect of a low waist line or hip band.

To provide as much length as possible in the skirt portion, let out the full width of the hem and finish the lower edge with a binding of self-material or of narrow ribbon, provided you carry out the trimming of ribbon on some other part of the dress, also.

Finishing the waist in Eton effect, dropping the skirt as low on the hips as possible, and adding a lower blouse portion and broad crushed sash of contrasting material is another possibility. In fact, if you wish to purchase contrasting material, you will undoubtedly be able to find a number of designs that will suggest a means of lengthening your dress, as the contrasting material may be inserted in horizontal rows in the skirt portion or in a broad band extending above and below the waist line and perhaps shaped in some odd manner.

Fashion Service Hat Frames

To copy the hats shown in Fashion Service, are we expected to make the foundation frames or can you supply them?
N. R.

If you have sufficient time and desire practice in frame-making, you should by all means make the foundation frames, particularly the skeleton ones used in the construction of transparent hats. However, if your time is limited, we would suggest that you purchase ready-made frames in order that you may have ample time for the making of your hat and not have to slight it in any way. Remember that exactness and good workmanship are extremely essential in the development of a successful hat, an accomplishment that is a joy to all women. We shall be glad to furnish you with frames for any of the hats that you decide to copy.

Straps and Cutouts for Footwear

Do you think that strap and colonial pumps will be worn very much this spring or is the plain pump coming back into favor? Also, what color would you advise me to get?
R. H.

Strap models are promised an overwhelming majority in footwear fashions, with the one-strap style leading and some attention given to two-strap pumps. With the tongue considerably diminished in size, the Colonial type is also included in footwear showings and the plain pump likewise is in evidence, but in numbers that seem insignificant in comparison with those of strap tendency.

Another feature that stands out very prominently is the vogue for cut-outs, this evidently inspired by old-time sandals. Evidence of this is found in tailored and sports models as well as in the dressier footwear and in modernized true-sandal types.

As to color, consider the costumes and uses for which you will need the pumps and select a color that will appear best for all these purposes. Fashion leans to footwear that matches the costume, but if one pair of pumps must be worn with a variety of costumes, black is the safe selection. Even with black pumps, you may carry out the color scheme of your dress in sheer silk stockings or, if this is a color that is too conspicuous for hose, wear light gray or beige stockings.

You might consider, also, the purchase of gray or tan suède pumps, as they appear harmonious with many colors and provide a pleasing change from black.

Want to Get Acquainted?

The following Institute students desire to become acquainted with other Institute students residing in their localities:

Sandusky County, Ohio...................A. M. B.
Brighton, Mass. (Telephone No. Brighton 3617R) C. C.
Chicago, Ill..............................N. M. M.
Philadelphia, Pa........................J. M. S.
Normal or Bloomington, Ill...............M. B. W.
Appleton, Wis...........................W. K.
Nevada, Iowa............................A. E. W.
Barnstead, N. H.........................L. B. P.
Pullman, Wash...........................E. McK.
Wisconsin...............................K. C. M.
Carl Junction, Mo. (Graduates)..........M. Y.

The following students would like to get in touch with other Institute students desiring partners or assistants:

WANT PARTNERS

Abilene, Texas (Dressmaking)................V. W.
Philadelphia, Pa. (Millinery)...............L. K.
Dent, Minn. (Graduates of Complete Dressmaking Course)..................................B. P. S.

WANT EMPLOYMENT

Wisconsin (Dressmaking)....................R. H.
Havre de Grace, Md. (Dressmaking)........E. M. C.
El Paso, Texas.............................L. M. S.
Chicago, Ill. (Dressmaking)...............C. E. R.
Miami, Fla. (Dressmaking—Children's Clothes)..............................E. H. W.
Los Angeles, Calif. (Dressmaking) .P. A. W.
Hibbing, Minn. (Dressmaking)....W. A. R.

I should like to become acquainted with students living in Tallahassee or Quincy, Fla.
MRS. ALICE CORRY WILHOIT,
208 Duval St.,
Quincy, Fla.

I should like to have Institute students in the vicinity of Long Beach, Calif., call on me.
MRS. VICTOR ERICKSON,
2500 Glendale Ave.,
Long Beach, Calif.

Millinery students living in the vicinity of Pittsburgh, Pa., are invited to attend the meetings of the Inspiration Club of that region, which was announced in the February, 1923, Inspiration. Kindly get in touch with Mrs. Bertha E. Edwards, telephone number Schenley 4224, or with Mrs. Amy Potts, telephone number Hiland 3815J.

I should like to become acquainted with a student in Hinton, W. Va., who has completed, or nearly completed, the Dressmaking and Tailoring Course.
E. J. B.

I should like to get in touch with some one in Pennsylvania or Ohio who has a shop and would like to have me make things for her to sell.
G. E. P., Penna.

I should like to become acquainted with students in the vicinity of Portland, Maine, or in Massachusetts, who would like some help in plain sewing or who might know of a place where I could find such work. I am French and 21 years old.
A. L.

About a year ago I started my dressmaking shop here, which I call "The Please You Shop," and which is the only one of its kind in this city. Owing to death in the family, I am forced to dispose of my shop, and I should like to see some Institute student get it. Menomonie is a school town and there is good business here for some one. I shall be glad to hear from any interested student.
ROSE MOSS SMITH,
Menomonie, Wis.

If other Woman's Institute students would like to get in touch with the inquiring students, we shall be very glad to give the addresses.

"IF"

If you can dress to make yourself attractive,
  Yet not make puffs and curls your chief delight;
If you can swim and row, be strong and active,
  But of the gentler graces lose not sight;
If you can dance without a craze for dancing,
  Play without giving play too strong a hold,
Enjoy the love of friends without romancing,
  Care for the weak, the friendless and the old;
If you can ply a saw and use a hammer,
  Can do a man's work when the need occurs,
Can sing when asked without excuse or stammer,
  Can rise above unfriendly snubs or slurs;
If you can make good bread as well as fudges,
  Can sew with skill and have an eye for dust;
If you can be a friend and hold no grudges,
  A girl whom all will love because they must.
If sometime you should meet and love another,
  And make a home with peace and faith enshrined,
And you its soul—a loyal wife and mother—
  You'll work out pretty nearly to my mind
The plan that's been developed through the ages,
  And win the best that life can have in store;
You'll be my girl, a model for the sages—
  A woman whom the world will bow before!

—Submitted by a Student

Our Students' *Own Page*

Fashion Service

This, of all months, seems the ideal one for a bit of extra attention to new clothes in general and spring fashions in particular. For this is the month bringing Easter and, moreover, such an early Easter as to stimulate an especially timely planning of the entire spring wardrobe. That Easter frock or suit has probably graced the occasion so satisfactorily that it has won permanent favor as a dress-up outfit for spring, but now there are so many other clothes to be provided. Some of you business girls are doubtless planning fresh new dresses for office wear or smart costumes or dresses for the season's good-time events, and surely you mothers are busy with your own sewing and the little folks' outfits.

When similar problems came up in past seasons, your Fashion Service helped many of you to solve them, and just how substantially it helped, your letters themselves gave the most interesting evidence. There were letters from dressmaker-students telling of the value of the book in professional work; letters from business girls who are dressing better and saving time by following Fashion Service instructions; letters from our housewife-students in appreciation of the department for home dresses, as well as more elaborate gowns, and the pages of clothes for the children. Space will accommodate only a few of these acknowledgments, but with the Spring-and-Summer issue of the book now in your hands, I can think of nothing more inspiring than a glimpse into what some students have actually accomplished with the help of previous issues. In fact, you will notice that each excerpt I am including reflects the unique practical value of Fashion Service, and I am sure that this spring, with a more complete and more nearly perfect issue for your guidance, you will be able to tell us of even greater accomplishments than these letters show.

Saves $35 on Service Design

Those of you who still have the Fall-and-Winter 1922-23 Service on hand may easily refer to the Slenderizing Costume, 7D, which Mrs. Evelyn G. Wyman, a New Jersey member, chose as her model. Her worthwhile saving speaks for itself, but another point worth noticing is her original color combination, which should help materially in accentuating the desired slenderness of line. "I made the front and back of reddish paisley Canton," Mrs. Wyman writes, "and the sides of black Canton with the sections picoted together and the points picoted also. The dress cost me no more than $15 and I'm sure it couldn't be duplicated in any store under $50."

And another letter emphasizing the Service suggestions on made-overs ran: "I must offer you a bit of appreciation for Fashion Service. From the Spring-and-Summer number for 1922, I made a red plaid voile dress trimmed with black lace in panel effect and, though it cost only $2.25, every one remarked how lovely it was. Then, this fall I was despairing of making over a really lovely old tweed dress of mother's for myself when along comes Fashion Service with a solution on the Economy-Dress page. It does help so much to find designs like that."

School Girl Makes Fashion Service Dress After 5 Lessons

Last spring, one of our school-girl students from Tennessee had completed only 5 lessons of her Dressmaking Course. How much good she derived from them, however, is evidenced first by her high grades, all between 96 and 100, and then still more substantially by the well-made clothes she is wearing. "I can hold my head higher in school because I'm no longer ashamed of my clothes," her letter opened. "One little pongee dress which I made from the Spring-and-Summer Fashion Service is a particular favorite and I am complimented on it every time I wear it. Among the other dresses I have made is an organdie for my sister. Here, too, I used an idea from the Service. My sister lives in another town and to make it more difficult she is hard to please, but she wrote that she hadn't seen a dress she liked better."

With so ambitious and successful a beginning, one cannot help imagining how many clothes she has made since and how much money she has saved on them for herself and the other members of the family.

And right here I am tempted to add this expression of appreciation from the mother of one of our Texas girls: "I certainly appreciate your interest in Ruth more than I can tell. She has recently copied two beautiful dresses, one a red lawn trimmed in black lace, and the other a blue voile trimmed in wide white lace, both from your Fashion Service. Her friends say they are the prettiest dresses they've seen, notwithstanding we live at Forth Worth where Domestic Art is taught."

Finds Inspiration for Her Own Dress and Sister's Trousseau

"Just when my Fashion Service arrived," wrote Miss Davis, of Alberta, Canada, "I was trying to make up my mind about a little office dress, and as a delightful surprise I found an answer to my problem in model 7A. My material is navy tricotine and I made the insert the full length of the dress, using scarlet broadcloth. Then, for trimming, I added tiny buttons covered with scarlet. My mother was delighted and so was everyone at the office, especially when I told them I made the dress in three evenings.

"All summer long, after working hours, I sewed on my sister's trousseau. And how I loved it! She has never done a bit of sewing in her life and she wanted the daintiest underwear and the prettiest dresses. For her evening dress, I made a pale-pink period gown, nearly like one of the Fashion Service models with panels of white lace over chiffon Georgette. I made circles of bias strips and inserted cord, finishing each off with clusters of pale-pink, mauve, and yellow roses with the palest of green leaves."

Then came a description of the white satin wedding dress, continuing with: "I was my sister's maid-of-honor, so I chose for my dress a replica of another Fashion Service design. I developed it in pale-pink taffeta and trimmed it with rosebuds in the same manner as my sister's. Although my sister has been married over a month, people are still talking about the wedding. They all say they never saw a prettier wedding, and one of the ladies who was a guest has asked me to take charge of a sewing class of girls. And all this success I owe to the Woman's Institute. Please accept my appreciation for your wonderful assistance through Fashion Service."

For full information regarding Courses in Home or Professional Dressmaking, Millinery, or Cookery as taught by the Woman's Institute, address a letter or a post card to WOMAN'S INSTITUTE, Dept. 21, Scranton, Pa.

Fashion Service Invaluable to Dressmakers

Just how completely Fashion Service can remove the handicap of the small-town dressmaker is brought out clearly in this short note from another Canadian member, Mrs. T. V. Townsend.

"What a real 'Service' you are to us students who are so far from a fashion center. My customers, some of whom go regularly to Edmonton and Calgary, say they find newer ideas in Fashion Service than in the most exclusive shops there."

A similar tribute to the style value of the Service was brought out in the letter of Miss Alice Stainton, who is also doing dressmaking in a small town. Here is her letter in part:

"Before taking the course, I had done a great deal of sewing, but now I am gaining the confidence that I lacked and I have many better ideas of construction. I have a dressmaking shop in my own home village, and the other day a lady who gave me her work told me that it was so hard to get her work done properly in the next town, for the dressmakers there could give her no idea of what material to combine with what she had or the style that would be good for the combination. But in Fashion Service, I get my suggestions on all these things. No wonder my customers like Fashion Service and tell me the designs are so exclusive.

Completed Course But Values Service Instructions

Recently when Mrs. Zora McPhail, of Seattle, Washington, was reporting on the last lesson of the Complete Dressmaking Course, she gave us an interesting glimpse into the orders for outside sewing that her course, together with Fashion Service, enabled her to handle.

"Ever since I can remember," she writes, "I have been able to sew—in a way—but not knowing how to do things properly would often result in a nervous spell before I had finished my frock, and I simply couldn't afford ready-mades nor an expensive dressmaker."

Then she goes on to tell how she sent for information about the Woman's Institute, enrolled for the Complete Dressmaking Course, and, as she studied, found the correct, easy ways of doing the things that had troubled her. "I have no fear now," she continues, "of undertaking the most intricate garments of most expensive materials because I follow your advice concerning muslin models when in the least doubt. I am now on my last lesson and besides studying I have made 12 house dresses, 7 summer dresses, 7 evening gowns, 26 afternoon dresses, 1 tailored suit, and 1 cape. It is not so much the quantity as the quality I am proud of. These things were made for girls I knew at college, who usually paid more than I asked.

"Fashion Service has been a wonderful help to me. In fact, more than half the things I have made have been copied from it"

Fashion Service

SUPPLEMENT

Each Issue of *Vintage Notions Monthly* includes a *Fashion Service Supplement*. You will read about the fashion styles popular in the early twentieth century and receive a collectible fashion illustration to print and frame.

The students of the Woman's Institute would also receive a publication called *Fashion Service*. Where the *Inspiration* newsletter instructed them on all aspects of the domestic arts, not only sewing but also cooking, housekeeping, decorating, etc., *Fashion Service* was devoted entirely to giving current fashions with a key to their development.

Fashion Service prided itself on providing it's readers with reliable style information and the newest fashion forecasting. The publication wasn't just eye candy. The Institute stressed the importance of studying the fashions to benefit the sewer's understanding of dressmaking. To quote founder Mary Brooks Picken, "Once the principles of design...and of construction... are understood, beautiful garments will result. This publication comes to you as an aid to this desired goal. Read the text of every page and reason out the why of every illustration and description that your comprehension of designing and construction may be enlarged and your appreciation made more acute."

Today, these articles and illustrations give us a historically accurate view of what fashion really meant 100 years ago. Not only can we study these articles for an "of-the-time" style snapshot, but just as their students did, we can also learn to understand the principles of design and increase our sewing skills. In each issue, look for a collectible illustration in the back of the supplement!

Costume Suit

The three-piece suit fills so definite a place in the wardrobe needs of every woman that one looks confidently for its return each season. And each time it comes back in just a bit more attractive form than before. The design shown here has excellent balance, both in the completed costume for street wear shown in the large figure, and in the very attractive frock appropriate for afternoon wear, at the left, which is revealed when the coat is removed. It is truly a three-piece suit, since the blouse and the camisole skirt are two distinct garments.

Three-piece models usually choose for their development two contrasting materials—in some cases a combination of wool with a silk fabric. The fabric chosen for the model illustrated here is black crêpe satin, with the crêpe side used for the skirt, the coat, the dress collar, and the straight bands that appear in conjunction with the finely plaited sections. The satin surface is exposed in the blouse, the apron, the coat lining, the plaited trimming sections, the lining of the dress collar, and the ribbon-like belt that ties the coat snugly about the hips.

Trimming.—This model features several new trimming ideas. The contrast of the lustrous satin and the duller crêpe surface of the fabric is very attractive. Particularly effective are the plaited inserts and bands. The very striking effect of the embroidery motifs is brought about by the use of white and red Iceland wool. And, of course, no one would overlook the charm of the clever collar, which is cut in two pieces. The front section, which follows the shape of the neck line, is fastened to the blouse at the top, is loose at its lower edge, and joins the straight back section in a seam on each shoulder, the back section hanging loosely from the shoulder seams. The lining of the entire collar has the satin surface exposed, and the back section takes an unexpected turn which discloses this secret very charmingly. White fur banding, which may be purchased by the yard, forms the coat collar and cuffs.

Material and Pattern Requirements.—For a costume of this kind, 8 yards of crêpe satin should be provided. Of the fur banding, 1½ yards will be needed, and for the embroidery, 6 skeins of the white wool and 2 skeins of the red.

McCall pattern 3654 will serve admirably for the blouse portion of this suit. However, you may not find it necessary to use a pattern for the blouse since it is so simple. The only shaping is in the slope of the shoulder seam and the neck outline. The under-arm seam is perfectly straight from armhole to hip and the fulness is disposed of in an inverted plait over the hip on each side. This plait is, of course, made before the plaited banding is applied.

The skirt, too, is very simple, McCall pattern 3540 being used if desired. The only change necessary will be to use only part of the tunic pattern for the apron. The necessary hip fulness is confined in a dart, which the very edge of the apron conceals. The apron is merely a length of the material 36 inches wide, with the fulness arranged on the hips. Both the skirt and the apron are attached to a long-waisted camisole of china silk. To keep the straight line at the bottom of the apron, it is necessary to drop the upper corners 1 inch below the camisole and stitch it to the skirt, gradually tapering the line up to the camisole toward the front.

For the coat, McCall pattern 3619 may be adapted by cutting off the belt-like band section.

Finishing.—The cuffs and hip band on the blouse are lined with straight pieces of the fabric, which help materially in keeping the plaits in place by relieving any strain that would come on them.

The neck of the blouse is finished with a bias facing. That part of it which is across the front effects the joining of the collar to the blouse.

The front section of the camisole top of the skirt has two darts at each under-arm seam to allow for fulness over the bust.

For the embroidery motifs on the coat and apron, chalk the design directly on the material, or trace it on tissue paper and baste this to the material. Work directly over the paper and pull it away when finished.

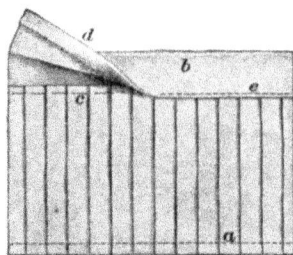

To make the plaited trimming, stitch the plaits across one edge, as at *a*. Baste the band *b* to the opposite edge, as at *c*. Turn it to the right side, fold down the edge *d*, and stitch, as at *e*.

Tricorne Modish for Tailleurs

Each new season the tricorne has been an item introduced in some form by a noted French designer. Up to the present time, these tricornes have been quite simple-patterned and modified after the Venetian mode, but this season they are having a more extensive use and are seen in more varied types.

In Model 7, a modified version of the tricorne, which is extremely modish for a tailleur costume, is shown. The shape is medium in size, with its coronet slashed in front and pinched down at each side. It is developed out of black, silky, straw allover, with the brim edge bound in No. 3 grosgrain ribbon. Vying most colorfully with the all-black fabric is a red-floss Chinese ornament used as a trim on the right side.

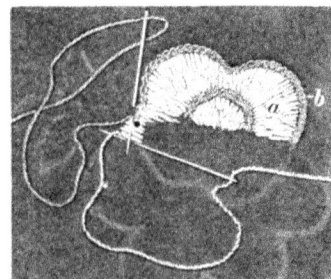

Using white Iceland wool, fill in the design with long and short stitches, as at *a*. Chain-stitch the edge with red Iceland wool, as at *b*.

Model 7

Coats and Suits

Model 7A.—Even coats are exploring the silky way, and who can wonder when such an attractive garment as this long straight-line model comes as a consequence of the exploration? Of black Roshanara crêpe, its trimming is limited to bandings of heavy picot-edged ribbon, those at the sides turning under at the lower edge. The loops at the ends of the collar and on the long set-in sleeves give a touch of individuality to these.

McCall pattern 3572 will make the development of this model very simple. For an average figure, 4½ yards of Roshanara crêpe, 4 yards of crêpe de Chine or Canton for lining, and 8 yards of ribbon will be needed.

Model 7B.—White linen is universally admired as a summer fabric, yet many object to it because of its tendency to wrinkle. This model solves the problem very well and adds to its charm at the same time by using cretonne for the skirt of the very attractive and practical straight-line dress. Then, to make the coat feel as though it is really a part of the ensemble, it is provided with collar, imitation pockets, and half sleeves of cretonne.

To make this model, 2¾ yards of cretonne and 3¼ yards of linen should be provided. For the dress, you may use McCall pattern 3597, and for the coat, McCall pattern 3181.

Model 7C.—Stellar satin is a newcomer in the realm of fabrics which has early attained considerable popularity. No more beautiful medium could be found for the expression of fashion's favorite coat features than this soft, lustrous material in black developed according to this design. Bandings of silk braid in varying widths form an unusual trimming and at the same time simulate a short jacket at the low waist line and give emphasis to the lower edge of the smart three-quarter length. A vertical band of the braid extends the full length of the back. There are no cuffs, but the braiding is an attractive substitute and entirely covers the collar.

The construction is simple and easily accomplished by using McCall pattern 3525 as a guide in cutting. For the average figure, 4½ yards of 40-inch satin and 3¼ yards of 40-inch lining will be necessary.

Model 7D.—Stucco, a tan with just the faintest pinkish cast, is the color used for this becoming three-quarter-length French model of soft wool. Bands of novel braid or embroidery in a simple band pattern developed in a slightly darker tone of embroidery silk, form the panel-effect decorations. Both the right and the left sides of the coat are exactly alike. There is a panel in the center back, one on each side in under-arm effect, and one at the center front of each side. The one on the left side is completely hidden by the overlapping of the right side.

It is quite all right for the highly original pockets to employ tan bone buttons and worked buttonholes to call attention to their smart new line. But no wrap would be quite up to last-minute smartness if it used buttons to effect a closing. The 1924 coat is merely wrapped around and held in place, cape fashion. However, snap fasteners are easily concealed and may be smuggled in.

Two lengths of 54-inch material and an equal amount of crêpe de Chine for lining will be sufficient material. Approximately 14 yards of banding is the trimming requirement. Pictorial Review pattern 1913 may be used.

Model 7E.—This boyish sports suit is practical and tailored without sacrificing daintiness, for what could be daintier than poudre blue linen with collar of white linen? The tube-line dress also has a white linen collar and white cuffs as well. Its tube line is further emphasized by the four groups of vertical pin tucks in the front. Pearl buttons fasten the double-breasted coat.

This model is lovely also when developed in lavender flannel with white flannel trimmings.

In cutting the coat, it is not necessary to cut a separate front facing. Merely fold back the material as far as desired and lay the pattern edge on the fold. Do not stitch down the inner edge of the facing.

For developing the dress, Excella pattern E1437 may be used by pinning the vest section of the pattern to the front before cutting, and then outlining the desired neckline. It is advisable to tuck the material before doing the cutting. The coat may be developed from Excella pattern E1145. Provide 5½ yards of 40-inch linen and ½ yard of white linen for the collars and cuffs.

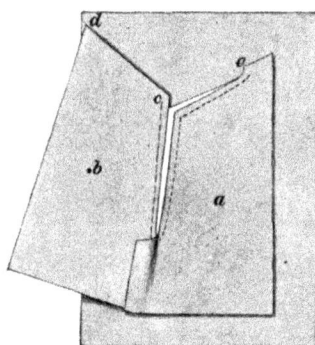

FIG. 1

Mark the pocket 7½×5 inches. Slash. Cut the front facing *a* as shown in Fig. 1 and the back facing *b* ½ inch larger each way. Place them, as shown, with the right sides of the facings and the coat together. Stitch along the slashed edges, as shown by the dotted lines. Bring *d* over to meet *e* and stitch together from *c* to *e*. Turn both facings to the inside, as in Fig. 2. Cut two

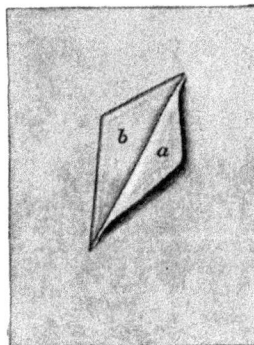

FIG. 2

more pieces the shape of *a*, Fig. 1, and 1 inch larger. Place the right sides together, stitch along the edges *a* and *b*, Fig. 3, and turn the seams inside. Insert this piece between *a* and *b*, Fig. 2, and, on the wrong side, stitch all the edges together to form the pocket. Work a buttonhole in *a*, Fig. 2, sew a button on the inserted piece, and button these together, leaving them loose from *b*.

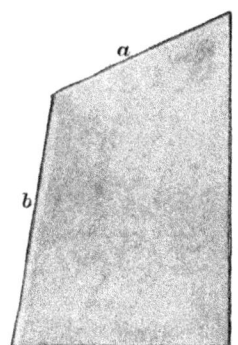

FIG. 3

7a

7b

7e

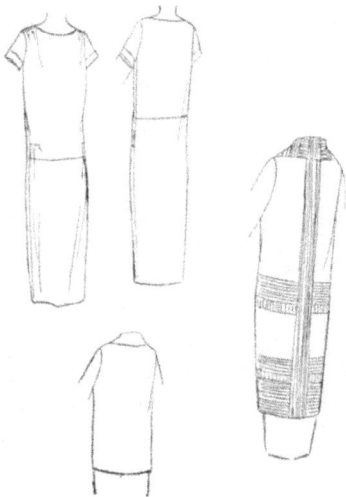

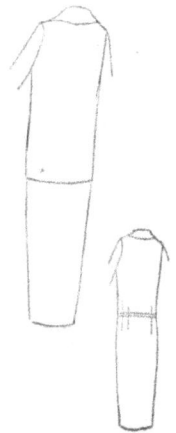

7c

7d

Blouses and Skirts

Model 8.—Boyish is the only word equal to the task of describing this blouse, which is quite the most popular of all the season's favorites. The front may be buttoned up and worn without the vest as in the little sketch.

Of printed crêpe de Chine or silk of novelty weave, 2¼ yards is sufficient. The vest and cuffs may be made from ¾ yard of organdie, net, or Georgette. McCall pattern 3608 is a good one to use.

Model 8A.—A popular selection for sports wear is this three-piece suit. The underblouse is of white dimity or crêpe de Chine with self-material plaited frills relieving its plainness. The skirt is of white silk-and-wool Canton crêpe cross-barred with ratiné-like threads of red. The sleeveless overblouse may be of red flannel or crêpe knit. Both overblouse and skirt have ribbon bindings.

McCall pattern 3575 may be used for the skirt, McCall pattern 3644 for the underblouse, and Excella E1423 for the overblouse. For the average figure, 1⅜ yards of 36-inch, or 1 yard of 54-inch material will make the overblouse; 2⅓ yards of crêpe de Chine, the underblouse; and 2⅛ yards of silk-and-wool Canton, the skirt.

Model 8B.—Rose handkerchief linen, with stitched-on bands of the same on the white vest and collar, fashions this smart, mannish blouse. To make it, 2¼ yards of rose and ½ yard of white linen should be provided. Pictorial Review pattern 2096 may be used.

Model 8C.—This is a type of blouse which makes a costume of a suit. It is made of crêpe satin, Canton crêpe, or plain or printed crêpe de Chine in a color to match the suit. A pattern is unnecessary since all pieces are straight, except those that form the sleeves, and they are shaped as shown in the small design. They may be straight at the top without even a shoulder seam. With very careful planning, it is possible to make the blouse from 1½ yards of material, but 2 yards is a safe estimate.

Model 8D.—Truly Parisian is this attractive "Mon Boy" dress. It derives its name from the figure of a man and the words "Mon Boy," which are outlined on one end of the tie.

Made of silk-and-wool Canton in log-cabin color, it is attractive with trimmings of green crêpe de Chine. Red or navy trimmings might be used, if preferred.

The necessary materials include 4 yards of silk-and-wool Canton, ½ yard of crêpe de Chine, 1⅓ yards of faille ribbon, 1¼ inches wide for the tie, and 1 yard of percaline for the sham. Use Style pattern S7671.

Model 8E.—Ribbon as a trimming is strongly emphasized on nearly every type of garment. Here, we have brown ribbon applied with blanket-stitching to a simple little kimono-sleeve blouse of tan silk crêpe whose fulness is buttoned in on the hips.

It is worn with a skirt of brown silk-and-wool crêpe that matches the ribbon in color. The skirt is very simple, being two straight lengths, not quite the full width of the material, gathered at each hip and attached to a long-waisted camisole. No pattern is necessary.

For the blouse, provide 1⅞ yards of crêpe, and for the skirt, two lengths and a hem allowance. Pictorial Review pattern 2115 will be helpful in developing the blouse.

Model 8F.—Very simple, and "just the thing" to wear with a gay sports blouse, is this skirt of flannel. The color, of course, should be chosen to harmonize with the blouse. The plait on each hip runs counter to tradition by turning toward the front.

McCall pattern 3574 would be a good one to use. Just two lengths of material are required.

Model 8G.—Ribbon woven through hemstitched slashes at the lower edge of this skirt makes the novel band trimming. A double or faced band of checked material will produce a similar effect. An attractive combination is reseda green Canton crêpe and white ribbon. Large pearl or self-covered buttons effect the closing.

McCall pattern 3562 may be used by cutting the opening where that pattern has a plait and making allowance for a front facing.

For the average figure, 2⅝ yards of Canton crêpe and about 10 yards of ribbon will be needed.

Model 8H.—Presented here is a sports dress that commands interest. The blouse may be patterned after Woman's Home Companion model 4441. The embroidery is simple. Squares with stitches radiating from the center are connected by chain-stitching. Black embroidery on white Shantung makes a striking combination.

The skirt is knife-plaited. For it, use a width equal to three times the hip measure. The blouse requires 2 yards of Shantung and 5 skeins of silk.

To have the plait in Model 8F loose its entire length, first stitch the hem, as at *a*, using blind-stitching in preference to machine stitching. Then fold the plait in place and stitch through the hem, to the extreme lower edge, as at *b*. Where the plait crosses the hem, there will be six thicknesses of material.

8B

8C

Model 8

8A

8E

8F

8G

8D

8H

Slenderizing Costume

Model 9.—This distinctive dress, especially designed for large figures, is essentially smart, yet its simplicity adds to its charm and helps in emphasizing every interesting detail. One instantly realizes, in thinking of this design for a large figure, that two essentials are achieved. In the panel, the crosswise picot-edged bands relieve the plainness and break the width across the front. And the trimming lines of ribbon give the required length lines, likewise a finish that is altogether desirable.

Picture, for a moment, how attractive this model would be in brown Canton with tan Georgette, in black moiré with gray Georgette, or in black satin with the dull side out for the dress and the shiny side for the tiered panel. No matter what the color,—gray, black, brown, navy, or tan—a dozen combinations of colors and fabrics suggest themselves, so that if one gives extreme care to all details a successful dress is sure to result.

For this model, 3 yards of 40-inch Canton crêpe, 1½ yards of the Georgette for the panel and sleeve trimmings, and 4 yards of ribbon or braid for banding are needed. Fashionable Dress pattern 3440 is almost an exact duplicate. However, any one-piece plain pattern can be used if one marks off the width desired for the front and the back panel.

For the front panel, the picoted pieces may be put directly over a plain piece of the Georgette and this sewed into the dress. Or, a foundation slip may be made and the picoted pieces fastened to this and the dress made free from the slip. In such an event, the picoted pieces should be wide enough to extend almost the full width of the front of the slip so that in walking the slip itself will not be visible.

The dress is very simple to make if the bands are marked evenly and hemstitched and cut neatly, and the dress cut and seamed, the seams pressed open, and the ribbon or braid band slip-stitched in place so that the fastening stitches will not be visible.

If a slight blouse is desired at the side waist line, a foundation slip is required. The dress may then be lifted up and pinned to the slip so as to allow for the blouse desired. Then, it should be tacked to the slip in several places and the belt brought over these tacking stitches to conceal them.

The lower section of the sleeve trimming is made deep enough to extend up to the sleeve itself, the second section is shorter, and the third one still shorter, so that when they are put together they make three tiers. The binding is used on the bottom of the sleeve and the Georgette neatly caught underneath the binding so that no stitches are visible on the outside.

Model 9A.—If a dress carrying dignity as well as being very simple and easy to develop is desired, this model should be chosen. Canton crêpe, crêpe de Chine, voile, Georgette, or any of the soft, clinging fabrics can be successfully used in developing a dress of this type. A full-length line is really achieved from neck to hem, varying slightly in its direction but still giving the effect of length. The surplice, with its long revers, is especially desirable for a large-bust figure. If the hips are narrow, the deep cuff shown here may be used, but if they are wide a smaller cuff should be chosen. It will be observed that the shoulder yoke, which is used here to allow fulness across the bust, is made to slant downwards so as not to cut the figure across the shoulders.

For this dress, use Excella pattern, E1361, which comes in sizes up to 52 bust. For medium-large figures, 4½ yards of 40-inch material, 1¼ yards of material for collar, cuffs, and cascade drape, 4½ yards of 1½-inch banding, and from ¼ to ⅜ yards of vesting are required.

Braid or ribbon may be used for the banding, but it must be soft in order that it will fall gracefully. On a summer dress, lace or the attractive footing that is used so much on handkerchiefs would make an effective trim. For instance, if the dress were of gray dotted voile, the collar and cuffs and cascade drape could be of white and the banding of gray or blue footing, either of which would be effective and smart.

The vest may be of lace or tucked net and it may be attached to the dress by means of snap fasteners or fastened directly to the slip and the dress allowed to fall free over it.

The dress should be seamed up, fitted, and finished, and then the collar and cuffs and the cascade piece made and applied in the last fitting. This plan will save time in the making and will insure the trimming pieces being exactly right.

Decoration or trimming requires consideration when used for a stout figure, for there is always danger of its emphasizing size. And since simplicity is the fashion, why decorate unless wisely? A dress, to be simple, need not be plain and sack-like, for it can be so cut and made as to be ultra smart.

Deep Side-Roll Featured

Elegance combined with smart simplicity is the theme followed in Model 9, Baronet haircloth, accordion plaited, embodies all the attributes of richness as well as being easily applied to the deep brim without an appearance of bulkiness. The Second Empire period is the source of inspiration for the decided brim roll at the left side and the rather high crown.

This model may be developed in a solid color or a combination of colors to match the gown or in a contrasting color to brighten up a dark dress.

The plaited haircloth is drawn around the brim edge and shaped into the head-size on top and underneath. A row of fluted ribbon is applied around the edge. For the crown, the plaiting is laid around the side and shaped to conform to its outline. A cocarde made of the plaiting and ribbon is attached low at the right side, making a very attractive self-fabric trim.

Model 9

9a

Variations of Slenderizing Costume

Model 9B.—Especially desirable for the young, large woman is this tiered model with long waist. It has youth, dignity, and a simplicity of line that does not emphasize size. The panels in the front and the back allow of fitting and at the same time give lengthwise lines that are ever advantageous in a dress of this type. These panels may have ribbon or novelty braid trimming or they may be hand-embroidered, as one desires. There are many beautiful braids to be had, which, if tastefully selected and applied, will add much to the value of a dress.

Tan Canton crêpe with embroidery in brown is the first suggestion. Poudre blue with black embroidery or brown with tan embroidery also is good for color. Any of the soft silks or linen would be very appropriate for material.

In applying tiers, as in this case, allow each tier to extend up under the one above at least 3 to 4 inches. In stitching the tiers flat to the foundation skirt, make just one turn of the material so that there will be as little bulk as possible.

Excella pattern E1395 makes a good guide for cutting and calls for just 4½ yards of 40-inch material.

Model 9C.—The woman who dresses well season after season, who is quite as successful in clothes selection as in her housekeeping, knows the virtue, value, and satisfaction of dotted voile or Swiss. Navy blue with white dots proves an old standby.

Here we have green voile with white dot and white voile collar and cuffs edged with narrow baby Irish lace. All the requisites of a summer dress are combined in this model—it is cool, becoming, attractive, and simple enough in line to tub often if necessary. The shirtwaist blouse and straight skirt are plain in themselves, but with the Tuxedo collar, the cuffs, the vestee, and the skirt panels, the plainness disappears completely.

In a dress of this kind, a generous hem is an advantage, it often being made 12 or 14 inches deep. Sheer materials require either deep hems, bound lower edges, or some form of decoration that will balance well with the rest of the dress. A large person should always avoid hems that are less than 3½ inches wide, as well as an appearance of stinginess in any proportion.

Excella pattern E1358 may be used for cutting. When you buy material, purchase 4¾ yards of voile and 5 yards of lace edging.

Model 9D.—Linen, ratiné, especially the silk ratinés, and any of the soft wools or novelty suitings immediately suggest themselves as fabrics suitable for such a design as this. 'Tis easy to picture the smartness of mocha linen, for instance, with écru linen collar and cuffs and bindings and with tie of brown ribbon, or mellow yellow ratiné or suiting with cream trimmings and brown tie.

The dress, in appearance a semisuit, may easily be cut from a plain one-piece dress pattern. The upper part of the skirt comes up slip fashion under the jacket portion, which may be sewed in with the under-arm seam or bound, in keeping with the front edge, and left free at the under arm. This model may take on a very new fashion effect if the slip portion is made of checked or plaid wool or silk and the jacket portion made complete in itself, with the back cut as long as the front, and worn over the slip. The one precaution in doing this is to keep a slender and definitely straight effect, allowing neither skirt nor jacket to flare even the least little bit. If an accurate pattern is desired, use Le Bon Ton pattern 52.

Approximately 4¼ yards of plain material, with ⅓ yard of trimming, 1 yard of ribbon for the tie, and a card of a dozen pearl buttons will make the dress.

Model 9E.—Wash silk is always a delight—whether for lingerie or for frock. Here we have a very distinctive dress, slenderizing in its possibilities, becoming, and yet simple enough in line to be truly desirable. Any of the smart wash silks, Canton, pongee, or gingham silk may be used for it.

The shirtwaist yoke is a 1924 note; in fact, so is the whole effect, for is it not easy to see that the skirt portion is just a continuation of the tailored blouse which is coming back with fervor this season?

The bias tie scarf and wristlets of contrasting color are interesting details, as are also the tab pockets and the buckles at the termination of the belt.

Woman's Home Companion pattern 4419, which is practically a duplicate, calls for 5½ yards of 40-inch material or 6½ yards of 32-inch fabric.

Model 9F.—Here we have a coat dress in silk—a novelty perhaps, but one that may be just as popular as the wool or linen one. In this case, the dress has a side opening to the shoulder, and is paneled in front and back to give additional line value.

Moss green Canton is used for this model, with 2-inch bands of darker green stitched flat to the dress. Over the bands, in running-stitch, is a design done in gold thread to give interesting decoration and to relieve the plainness of the bands. A bit of the embroidery is illustrated in the insert at the bottom of the page.

Pictorial Review embroidery pattern 12426 is good to use for this design. For the dress, Excella pattern E1413 may be used, this requiring 4½ yards of 40-inch material for a figure 42 to 46 bust.

This type of dress could be paneled with groups of pin tucks and the side fulness smocked in place. A V or boat neck and long, tight sleeves might be substituted.

For summer materials, lace insertion could be put in as inserts rather than the bands stitched on, or, in the striped silks or ginghams, crosswise bands could be applied.

9B

9C

9D

9E

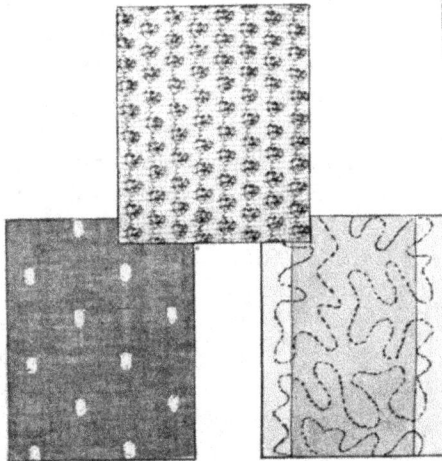

9F

Home Dresses

Clothes have a way of reacting on both the wearer and her associates to such an amazing degree that she who prizes harmony as a part of the daily life of her home will not grudge the little additional time necessary to plan and make a home dress worthy of expressing her personality. The great proportion of time spent in home dresses by home women causes them to assume marked importance. Not only must they be becoming, but they must be comfortable and practical as well.

Model 10.—A dress that measures up to the ideal in every way is this One Hour type. Made from such a fabric as cretonne, gaily sprigged with more or less conventional flowers in sunny gold, flame, reds, and tans, it can withstand the subduing influence of plain tan Everfast for the blouse portion. However, any favorite color may be used.

The fitted bands at the neck and sleeves and the plain-color pocket flaps are bound with brown of a darker tone than the blouse. The hip fulness is confined under narrow sashes, which are secured by large buttons and then tie in the center back. An 8-inch slash down the back will facilitate the removal of the dress.

To develop this dress, 1¼ yards of plain material, 36 inches wide, and 2¼ yards of cretonne will suffice. Before cutting the blouse, remove two strips 2¼ inches wide from the sides to serve for the ties.

Model 10A.—There is an elegance in simplicity which the discriminating woman seeks quite as earnestly in her home dresses as in her more formal apparel, and which is possessed in great measure by this model, made of rose Everfast or linen with white collar and cuffs edged with baby Irish lace. It needs only the hand drawn-work and darker rose French knots to raise it out of the commonplace.

For this model, 3½ yards of rose Everfast, ⅓ yard of white linen for collars and cuffs, 2 yards of lace, and 1 skein of embroidery floss will provide sufficient material. Excella pattern E1471 will help in its development.

Model 10B.—The long lines of the front panel, together with the deep V line of the neck, make this model particularly suitable for the stout figure, although it may be worn by the slender woman as well. The material is cotton print, or percale, in green and yellow. The collar and cuffs and appliquéd squares are white Hebrides cloth, and the bindings are of plain green. The thread used for the appliqué is of the same green as the bindings.

The material requirements include 4 yards of 32- or 36-inch material, ½ yard of white Hebrides cloth, 7 yards of bias tape, and 1 skein of embroidery floss. Pictorial Review pattern 2026 may be used.

Model 10C.—For the figure that requires a little more than the usual fulness over the bust, this model of blue-and-white cross-barred gingham, with its square yoke and gathers, will be admirable. To apply the effective bias facing to the front opening, baste the right side of the bias to the wrong side of the dress front. Mark the opening line on the material. Stitch ¼ inch from this line on both sides of it and let the seam gradually come to a V at the lower end. Cut through both the material and the facing on the marked line. Bring the facing to the right side, turn the edges under ¼ inch, and stitch. White voile fashions the hemstitched collar, cuffs, and pocket flaps.

This dress, for which Pictorial Review pattern 2078 may be used, requires 4 yards of 36-inch gingham and ½ yard of voile.

Model 10D.—A simple, little kimono-sleeve dress with a removable bib-like panel in the front of the waist is this brown-white-and-blue gingham with rickrack trim. The panel may be unbuttoned at the shoulder and omitted when desired. It is held down securely at the lower edge by the sashes, which are fastened to it and tie in a bow in the center back.

For the medium figure, provide 3⅞ yards of 32-inch gingham and 1 bolt of rickrack. McCall pattern 3347 may be used.

Model 10E.—Both dignity and charm combine with practicability to make this model desirable. Its collar, which continues in a surplice line to the belt, and its cuffs and pocket are of allover embroidery in an eyelet design. The dress material is plaid gingham combining pink, green, and white. The long lines and the yoke-line fulness, which is tucked at the shoulders, make it adaptable to the stouter figure. An advantage of the coat-like cut is that very little time is required to put on or remove the dress.

Provide 5 yards of 32-inch gingham and ¾ yard of 22-inch embroidery for the average figure. Excella pattern E1472 is suitable for this model.

Model 10F.—Youthful, smart, and of boyish simplicity is this becoming model, which might be quite as attractive for sports wear, if made of the proper materials, as it is for home wear, made as pictured in gray plaid gingham with orange and blue embroidered dots. Blue chambray bands make an attractive trim. Those on the collar continue down the front as a striking tailored closing. The gathers in the back of the skirt emphasize the low waist line.

For the average figure, 3½ yards of gingham and ¼ yard of chambray will make the dress. Woman's Home Companion pattern 4425 may be used.

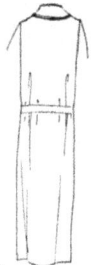
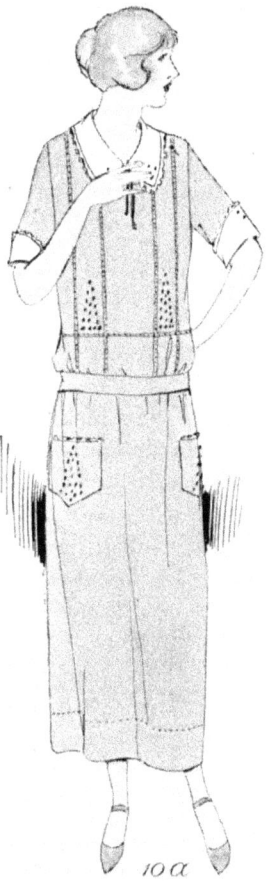

10 *a*

10 *c*

Model 10

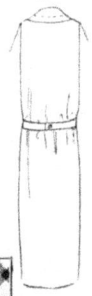

10 *e*

10 *d*

10 *b*

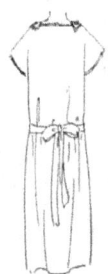

10 *f*

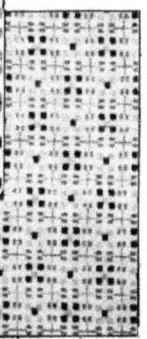

Junior Fashions

Model 11.—What could possibly be of greater importance in the world of the girl of Junior High School age than the matter of clothes? Her quest is for dresses that will reflect in some measure her own dignity, and it ends in glorious triumph when she comes upon this model of linen. For who would say that applied squares of self-material, hemstitched into position, or the daintily feminine touch of lace-edged white collar and cuffs would be in any wise unbefitting? Pin tucks and buttons accent her slimness and height.

For the blonde miss, no lovelier color could be chosen than poudre blue; for the brunette, any of the popular yellows; and for the lovely titian type, surely moss green is just the color.

Two lengths of linen are required with ¼ yard of white linen and 2 yards of lace for the collar and cuffs. Woman's Home Companion pattern 4434 may be used.

Model 11A.—Dainty as girlhood itself is this simple frock of orchid voile. Double bands of self-material cut straight and bound on the lower edge with white voile are attached by means of double hand hemstitching to the skirt, blouse, and sleeves. The neck and short slit in the front also are bound with white voile. Additional opportunity for hemstitching is found at the top of the deep hem and in three vertical rows in the blouse front. The rather wide belt is ornamented by rows of hand-run pin tucks and a bunch of lavender voile grapes with white organdie leaves.

Two lengths of voile, with allowance for a wide hem, and an additional ½ yard for bands should be supplied, as well as ⅓ yard of white voile for the bindings. Bits of cotton form the grape foundations. Pictorial Review pattern 1636 is very good.

Model 11B.—Tissue gingham of orange or tomato red with a bit of black and white in its plaid is lovely in basque effect with large bow and gathered pockets and neck trim of white organdie and the contrast of wee black velvet bows.

Only two lengths of gingham, 1 yard of organdie, and about 1⅔ yards of narrow velvet ribbon are required. If a pattern is desired, use Excella E1481.

Model 11C.—A mere slip, and practically sleeveless at that, is this simple yellow chambray dress, which depends for its smartness upon ap-plied in a panel design. One may cut flower motifs from cretonne, such as that photographed at the bottom of the page, and combine them, or secure a stamping pattern for the design.

Two lengths of material should be purchased. If a pattern seems essential, use Excella E1497.

Model 11D.—The revival of colonial tufted bedspreads has brought candlewick floss into use. The effectiveness and ease of working with this floss make it adaptable to other uses, and here is shown a clever use for it in combination with couching-stitch for ornamenting a dainty dress of pink crêpe de Chine.

Mark rows of dots ¼ inch apart where the tufting is desired. Then, with the floss double, pass the needle down into the material close up to the dot on one side of it, and bring it up on the opposite side of the dot. Run the thread from dot to dot, forming loose darning-stitches.

Cut in the exact center of each large darning-stitch. Brush with a stiff brush and trim any uneven tufts. French knots may be substituted for tufting, if desired.

McCall pattern 3605 may be used. About 4 yards of material, 1 or 2 skeins of mercerized cotton, and 1 hank of candlewick floss will be necessary for size 14 years.

Model 11E.—The brilliantly colored sleeveless coatee, with the plainly tailored natural-color pongee dress, gives just the amount of grown-up sophistication that the girl in her early teens desires in her sports clothes. In this case, the coatee is green silk ratiné bound with white grosgrain ribbon. Pearl buttons outline the pockets.

The coatee is so very simple that almost any blouse pattern could be used by flaring the under-arm seam slightly toward the hips. However, McCall pattern 3534 can be used for the coatee. The dress is similar to McCall pattern 2124. About 3 yards of pongee and 1¼ yards of the ratiné are needed for size 14 years.

Model 11F.—An adaptation of the One Hour type is seen in this smart dress of brown gingham cross-barred in white with embroidered dots of blue. It will appeal to any girl because of the fob pocket, which is one of Fashion's latest capers, and the simple "Johnnie" collar. The trimmings are of blue gingham.

Approximately 4 yards of plaid and ⅓ yard of plain blue gingham will be required.

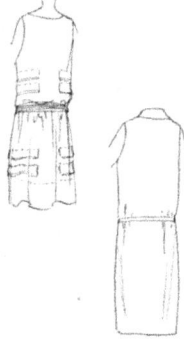

11 A

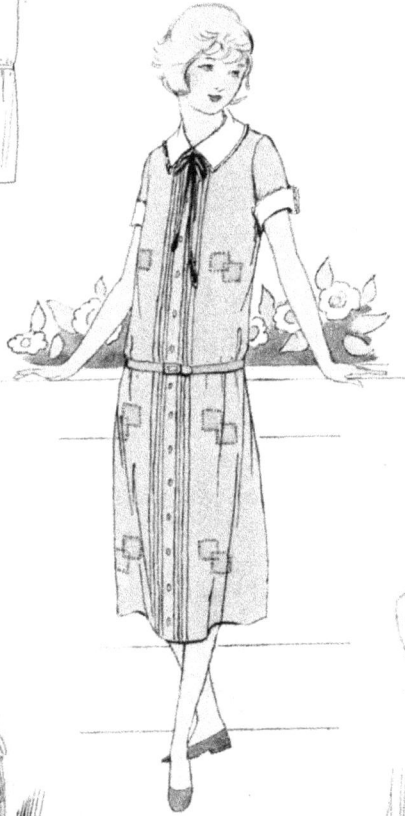

11 B

Model 11

11 C

11 D

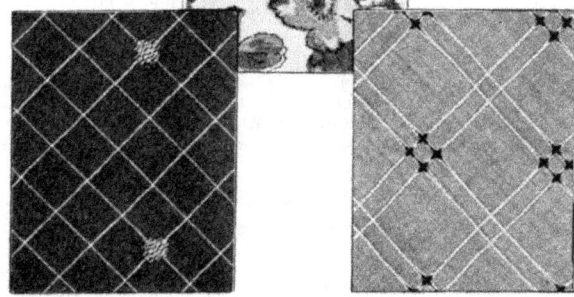

11 E

11 F

Children's Styles

Model 12.—"Everything like mother's," seems to be the aim of the 1924 child's wardrobe. And with everything in mother's wardrobe so simple and withal so pleasing, isn't the aim a worthy one? At least it has been achieved in this little tailored dress of orange linen with trimming bands and collar of natural linen. There is something in the bright gaiety of orange which seems to require a subduing touch of black somewhere to give it just the proper accent. In this instance, the accent takes the form of simple stitches between the bands of trimming, and a small black tie with flying ends.

The dress may be cut by any simple, kimono-sleeve pattern, such as Pictorial Review pattern 2069, out of two lengths of material and ½ yard of trimming.

Model 12A.—Just how little is required to raise a simple style out of the commonplace is shown by this one of pink-and-white novelty check print, which began as a perfectly plain little apron-like affair but took on an air of distinction that cannot be overlooked when inserts and pockets and cuffs of plaited white organdie were added to it. The plaits are not stitched—they are merely pressed. To hold them in place and to give a firm foundation for the tiny pearl buttons that trim the top of the pockets and the edge of the cuffs, a narrow tape or a band of organdie is attached to the wrong side, preferably by hand, so that the stitches won't show.

One might use McCall pattern 3602. Two lengths of the print and ½ yard of organdie will be sufficient.

Model 12B.—Blue-and-white tissue gingham and plain blue Everfast fashion this dainty dress, which gives a suggestion for the use of two remnants. For a child 8 years old, 1¼ yards of gingham and ¾ yard of Everfast will be enough material. By making allowance for the side plaits, one may use Pictorial Review pattern 2112.

Model 12C.—This simple coat, having as its chief attraction a collar that becomes a scarf at will, is very smart made in reseda green wool crepe with novelty buttons as its only trimming. Or, if one prefers tan wool crepe, red buttons will give chic contrast.

For an 8-year old girl, 2¾ yards of 36-inch wool crepe and a similar amount of crepe de Chine for lining will supply the material requirements, and for the pattern, Excella E1502 may be adapted.

Model 12D.—For her daintiest dress, no choice would please the girl from six to ten more than this charming one of white and peach-color voile. The hand embroidery gives evidence of thoughtfulness; but the novel effect gained by slashing the skirt at the hips, and the sleeve at the bottom, then rounding off the corners, binding the slashes with peach voile, and securing them to the belt and sleeve bands with tiny pearl buttons—this bespeaks real originality. There are four tabs on each hip and three on each sleeve. The applied hem of peach voile is secured with hemstitching.

For the 8-year old size, provide 1¾ yards of white and ¾ yard of peach voile. Pictorial Review pattern 1076 may be used for foundation lines.

Model 12E.—This ribbon-trimmed dress of pink voile or crêpe de Chine is characterized by distinctive simplicity. The ribbon is blue and pink of the two-toned variety and each tiny loop is held in place by a small pearl button. Three plaits at each side front relieve the plainness and add fulness to the brief skirt.

For size 8, 2¼ yards of material, 3¾ yards of ribbon, and 1 dozen pearl buttons will be needed. McCall pattern 3636 is similar.

Model 12F.—Every girl, large or small, loves the unrestricted freedom of movement which the middy dress permits. There are times, however, when one feels that the galatea type is not quite appropriate. For such occasions, a dress such as this model, made of sea-blue crêpe de Chine with trimmings of white crêpe de Chine, will prove very welcome.

For the skirt, provide a width equal to three times the hip measure. For the blouse, twice the desired length will be enough, and ½ yard of white crêpe de Chine will supply trimmings. McCall pattern 3564 may be used.

Model 12G.—Add to the charm of childhood the piquancy of plaid gingham and the combination is quite irresistible. In this instance, the gingham is pink-and-white tissue, its daintiness being accented by trimmings of white organdie joined to the bias-front panel, the odd little collar, and the sleeves by entre deux.

A little more than two lengths of gingham, 3½ yards of entre deux, and ⅓ yard of organdie are needed. Pictorial Review pattern 2060 can be used.

Simplicity in Youthful Styles

Unlimited variety prevails in millinery for children from the simplest little hat meant for service and knock-about wear to the more frilly ones for "dress-up" occasions. On the opposite page are a few practical models, which are youthful expressions of the styles featured for the grown-ups.

Models 12 and 12G are youthful editions of the short-back cloche with high crown and simple tailored trim. These hats, as well as those in Models 12B and E, may be developed of visca, crêpe, or shot taffeta in one color or a combination of colors.

The jaunty tam in Model 12C, always a favorite with girls little and big, is made of straw yardage in a tone harmonizing with the coat. For dress-up wear, the long-front poke of hand-crocheted milan in Model 12D has a half-facing and scarf of Georgette. In direct contrast is the knock-about Breton in Model 12A of two-tone, hand-blocked milan hemp.

12 A

Model 12

12 B

12 C

12 D

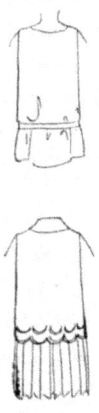

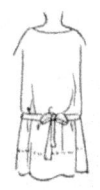

12 E

12 F

12 G

Tiny ~ Tot Styles

Model 13.—Simplicity is a coveted quality of the season, which is just as desirable in juvenile apparel as in any other wardrobe. This little model of flesh voile and lace has the art of being very simple and at the same time appearing rather intricate.

Two lengths of voile and about 3 yards of insertion and 2 yards of lace will be required. If a pattern is desired, use Pictorial Review pattern 2090.

Model 13A.—Rompers seem almost to have become the uniform of the American child for play time. They are being made of gingham with hat to match and are lovely in a tint to suit the child's own coloring. Another and a very new development is to make them of dimity, smocked in mixed pastel colors.

For a 2-year-old child, 1⅝ yards of 32-inch material will make this model. For the rompers, use McCall pattern 3625, and for the hat, McCall pattern 3612.

Model 13B.—Whether the popular flower-sprigged or dotted dimity or figured crêpe de Chine is chosen for this bloomer dress and matching hat, the result is bound to be pleasing. As shown here, the material is crêpe de Chine, and the trimmings are red crêpe.

McCall pattern 3640, which is similar, requires, for size 4, 2⅛ yards of material 32 or 40 inches wide. For the hat, one may use McCall pattern 3611.

Model 13C.—Heavy cotton of dull green makes the trousers in this model, which are buttoned to a white blouse of thinner cotton or handkerchief linen with a touch of smocking in the same green. The contrast in color is important because it draws attention to the fact that the two garments are separate and bear no resemblance to rompers.

McCall pattern 3340 is somewhat similar and may be adapted. In size 4, the blouse requires 1⅛ yards of 36-inch material, and the trousers, 1 yard.

Model 13D.—A bloomer dress may, after all, be quite as charming as any other if it relies on taffeta or organdie to express its charms. Then, with a touch of embroidery added, its success is assured.

One could scarcely find a better way to make one of the dainty new figured dimities than this. Or voile in pastel coloring would be appropriate.

McCall pattern 3577 is very much like this

model, and requires, for size 4, only 2¼ yards of 32-inch material.

Model 13E.—Tan soisette for the blouse and brown Everfast for the trousers make a splendid selection for this little two-piece suit. The blouse is double-breasted in effect and has a round collar and comfortable short sleeves. If there is a question as to the masculinity of plaited frills, use bindings of the darker color.

The construction is simple and Pictorial Review pattern 8989 may be used. For the blouse, 1⅛ yards of 36-inch material will be needed, and 1 yard for the trousers, if the boy is 4 years old.

Model 13F.—A tiny girl is always lovely in white organdie, but although it is dainty it lacks a certain piquancy which just a touch of color will give. Add, then, a laced-edged collar and two bands of red-dotted, white Swiss, as here, and the picture is complete. The bands are inserted in the skirt with narrow entre deux. Pin-tucked bands trim the tiny sleeves and the bloomers.

To use McCall pattern 3559 for making the dress, first tuck the material that is to be the front of the dress. Then pin the plaits of the pattern in place before cutting. Size 4 requires 2¼ yards of 36-inch material.

Model 13G.—The durability of pongee and the ease with which it launders, together with the delightful range of colors that can be bought, make it an ideal fabric for children's wear. The little suit shown here is made up in blue pongee with natural pongee trimming.

It is slashed at the left center front to give ample room for slipping on over the head. It is also finished at the lower edge for closing.

For size 4, 1⅝ yards of blue and ⅓ yard of natural pongee are needed. Use Pictorial Review pattern 1754.

Model 13H.—Smocking is as popular as ever for tiny tots' dresses. It is done in a contrasting color, or in a mixture of harmonizing colors. As shown here, the little sleeveless bloomer dress is of blue-and-white tissue gingham with smocking in black. But flowered dimity with mixed smocking would be lovely.

The simulated sleeves are merely straight bands of the material applied to the armhole. When cut by McCall pattern 3556, size 4 requires 2¼ yards of material that is 36 inches wide.

Hatting the Tiny Tots

In kiddies' millinery, where comfort is of chief importance, all rigid styles are barred, the hats being made unsupported except for a narrow head-size band. This feature is emphasized in the models shown on the opposite page.

Models 13 and 13H follow the lines of mother's tiara toque, the crowns in one- or two-piece effect and the off-the-face brims highest in the center front. Taffeta and flat visca are the popular fabrics for these "best" hats, while a flat appliquéd floral design on the brim or bunches of fine flowers around the crown make a smart trimming.

For play, the tub hats, youthful versions of the cloche and cuff brim, as shown in Models 13A and B respectively, are developed in the same material as the frocks, as are also the quaint little pokes in Models 13D and F.

13 A

13 B

13 C

13 D

13 E

13 F

13 G

Model 13

13 H

Millinery Fashions

From the endless array of models furnished by the Parisian designers for spring and summer wear, there have emerged certain items in shapes, materials, and trimmings, which have met with sufficient approval to pronounce them the authentic modes.

Comfort exerts such a strong influence in modern fashion ideals that the small hat presents a logical expression of what truly smart women desire to complete the perfect silhouette of slenderness. And, too, the accepted coiffure favors this type of hat, for the tight hairdress and shingled bob require a close-fitting hat even for midsummer wear. Though medium brims and fairly large affairs are in the minority, they are endorsed and shown by a goodly number of authoritative designers.

The mysterious reddish, greenish, and bluish tones, so aptly used by the Orientals in their choicest art, are the last word in color. They form striking harmonies with the new yellow and orange hues, and also with the flame-tinged melon and crab-apple shades. From the Far East the pursuit for colors is followed to America, where the rich art of the early Indian tribes yields beautiful colors, such as the warm, rose-tan tones of Maya and Mexico, and the more neutral tones of a light tan called lariat and a rich brown known as cowboy. Then, the soft and subtle tones of delicate blue, the rosy coral pink, and the amethyst shades so much favored in the days of the Second Empire, are found in large quantities for midsummer wear.

Retaining their uninterrupted reign of popularity, the visca allovers imitate everything in their new straw weaves, from faille and crêpe to moiré, satin brocades, and other intricate effects. While there is a decided tendency toward blocked hats, and particularly blocked crowns with fabric combinations for the brims, many of the large straw body hats employ gold- and silver-cloth facings as well as unique ribbon effects.

Ribbon is to play a stellar rôle in the styles of the coming season. It is used in every imaginable way, not only as trimming, but for making entire hats. This idea in itself is not new, but there are so many different kinds of ribbon and such remarkable color blends that the results obtained are totally different from anything ever attempted before. Color combinations score when embroidery is the issue—a perfect blending, but not a single color dominance.

Flowers of all kinds are considered definitely the trimmings for spring and summer hats, very clever novelties being devised. Varieties that never grew in either garden or forest are marvels in coloring and artistic in the extreme. American beauties, morning glories, and poppies have their petals hand-colored in the most unusual ways. Small flowers in brilliant colors are used for the solid covering of crowns or brims.

Long, slender leaves of leather, ostrich, and other plumage, with their edges tipped in gold or silver paint, are popular novelties. Whether plumage or flowers form the trimming of a hat, it should be arranged so as to conform to the line of the hat.

Model 14

14 a

14 B

14 C

14 D

BRETONS that roll easy off-the-face, permitting unique innovations of under-brim treatments, are destined for a long and uninterrupted run. This feature is evidenced in Model 14, where small button daisies in soft rose tones are appliquéd flat for the facing. Grosgrain moiré visca in navy blue is used to cover the top brim and rather high bell crown. A band of narrow ribbon finishes the base of the crown.

Capelines, very wide and somewhat droopy of sides, are confined principally to the more dressy modes, as shown in Model 14A. Here, the brim is outlined with a pendant maline flange, which softens the edge of a blocked brown timbo. Changeable watermelon taffeta is used for the underfacing and side crown. Clustered at the right side front is a spray of ostrich flowers in colors matching those of the hat.

Pokes in variation are attracting considerable notice, both those of the regulation type and off-shoots of the original line, as shown in Model 14B. A Neapolitan plateau is used for the top brim with one layer of maline for the facing, finished on the edge with a triple cord of ciré satin. A transparent crown of black maline has lace draped horizontally over the crown, which falls off at the right in a long scarf effect. A ciré satin collar, narrow in the front and wide across the back, completes this unusual version of the poke.

Cloches have been the theme for so long that there is little left to say about them except that they are becoming practically brimless, as shown in Model 14C, the result being the cloche-toque. Developed in black haircloth, the mere suggestion of brim and side crown is covered solid with bronze, gold-edged foliage applied in regular rows. Relieving the severeness is a cluster of varied-size loops of black moiré ribbon attached rather low at the right side.

Directoire influence, inspired by the hats of both men and women of the Second Empire, is beautifully expressed in Model 14D. Medium in size, with a flaring front and sharply upturned slashed back brim, this model partakes of the high square crown and thus embraces every feature of the Directoire type. It is a hand-blocked milan with an underfacing of rose color gros de Londres. High in the center front, a bunch of American Beauty roses is applied to give height.

Look for a collectible print version at the end of this issue.

Distinctive Hat Modes

Model 15

15 C

15 D

15 a

15 B

Model 15.—Lariat grosgrain with a green tinsel corded edge is sewed spirally on this medium-sized brim. Green Georgette crêpe makes the plain facing, while the high oval crown is divided from front to back and the ribbon is applied to follow this line, giving the effect of two huge cocardes. On the right side, the last four strips to be attached are allowed to hang in long streamers.

Model 15A.—This tiny poke-cloche of tagal and faille combination in Maya color has a six-sectional crown of tagal piped in a deeper tone of faille. The small side-dipping brim is covered with the silk, which makes a pencil edge also, while a twin wreath of variegated flowers encircles the crown. From under the flowers and hanging just to the tip of the nose is a perky little lace veil.

Model 15B.—A happy combination that is much in favor is the large leghorn brim with a slight roll at the left side and the solid crown of flowers. Tiny forget-me-nots in variegated Chinese coloring of yellow and blue make the entire crown and a wreath of large purple pansies encircles its base. A 1-inch tuck of self-color maline is attached around the brim to produce a double-edge effect.

Model 15C.—Plaid visca cloth in a soft green, gold, and black combination is the fabric selected to cover the high oval crown and the top of the wide-at-the-sides and turned-up-back brim of this model. Black grosgrain moiré visca is used for the plain fitted facing and wide moiré ribbon makes the broad bow.

Model 15D.—Delightfully cool and refreshing is this long-front, face-shading poke so suggestive of vacation time. Pale yellow Canton is used to cover the entire hat, which is finished on the edge with a triple cord ranging from yellow to deep orange. Georgette in the same sunshine shades forms the drape around the crown and the long shoulder scarf, and large celluloid rings serve as a finish.

16 a

16 C

Model 16

16 B

16 D

Model 16.—The eternal smartness of black and white is exemplified in this close tailored effect, with its tiara cuff brim rolled up softly in the front and covered smooth with white Canton. Black visca braid makes the crown. A fob of brilliants and a fine lace veil are unique trimming touches.

Model 16A.—Entirely transparent is this all-black, tiny mushroom droop. The 2-inch brim is made of maline, and the edge is bound with moiré ribbon. Fine black lace, having one edge bound with moiré ribbon, is draped to form a high coronet and an off-the-edge drop.

Model 16B.—In pheasant color, this soft, timbo-chain body hat is faced with Mexico color maline, which is twisted to give the thick-edge finish. Sprayed loosely around the oval crown are colorful field flowers, including poppies, daisies, bluets, and natural color wheat and showing exceptional effectiveness in coloring.

Model 16C.—Cosmos coloring, from the deep purple to the pinkish lavender tones, dominates in this model. A purple tagal plateau makes the top brim and crown tip, while cosmos faille fits the facing and the side crown.   Silk leaves with padded pods of the several tones trim the side crown.

Model 16D.—Again, all-black glacé haircloth in plain and accordion-plaited combination makes this chic poke whose brim turns up in a deep collar effect across the back. Its quartered crown has two sections of plain and two of accordion-plaited haircloth. Burnt peacock outlines the collar.

Magic Pattern: Casual Jersey Blouse

▶▶▶ TRICOT JERSEY in nylon or rayon, or tubular wool jersey is suggested for this blouse. It requires ¾ yd. of 60-in. fabric. The diagram is given for the tricot, but the procedure is almost identical for the wool.

Straighten both ends of fabric. With fold toward you, overlap edge of top piece one-half the bust measurement plus 7 in. from fold, and pin along this edge.

From corner point A measure shoulder-to-waist length plus 4 in. to locate B. C is one-fourth bust measurement plus 1 in. above A. D is one-half armhole measurement plus 3 in. to right of C. E is same distance in from left-edge corner. F is one-half wrist measurement plus 2 in. to left of E. For G, measure up from A one-sixth neck measurement plus ½ in. I is same amount to right of A. Mark front neck curve from G to I. Form sleeve by drawing lines F to G, E to D. Place H one-fourth bust measurement plus 1 in. above B. Draw underarm line straight from D to H. Connect H with B. Cut I to G, G to F. Cut E to H, curving underarm at D, as shown. Cut H to B. This gives you front of blouse. Lay this over back section, ⅜ in. in from lengthwise edge and cut back, but do not cut back neck.

Seam center-back, using a ⅜-in. seam and beginning 8 in. down from top. (The tubular jersey needs no back seam.) Join shoulder seams, leaving 4 in. opening each side of neck.

From cutoff end pieces, cut facings for neck, as at J. Lay these pieces on, right side of facing to right side of blouse. Stitch a piece to neck front and back. Stitch front facing to shoulder opening in line with shoulder seam, as at K. Stitch back piece on, making ¼-in. seam on each side, as at L, so that back extends under edge of front on each side and seams appear continuous. Clip back shoulder seam, as at M, and clip seam edges on curves as shown.

Bring facing to wrong side. Turn outside edge under and stitch free of blouse, as in N. When pressed, facing will hold in place even without tacking stitches.

Clip underarm seam at curve. Hem bottom of blouse, using narrowest possible hem. Turn edge ⅛ in. at bottom of sleeve; stitch. Turn a ½-in. hem and slip-stitch.

Sew loops and buttons or snaps on neck openings. Press blouse carefully.

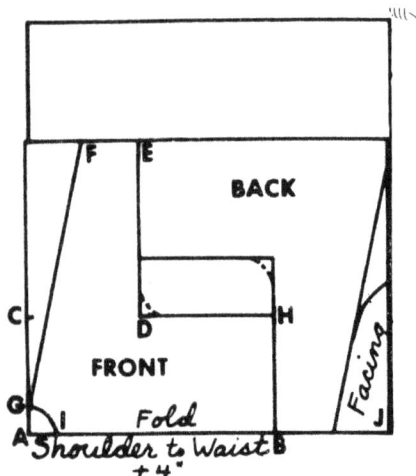

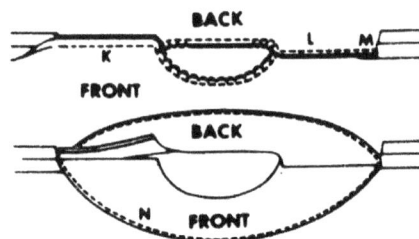

Your Measurement Chart & Notes on Making Magic Patterns

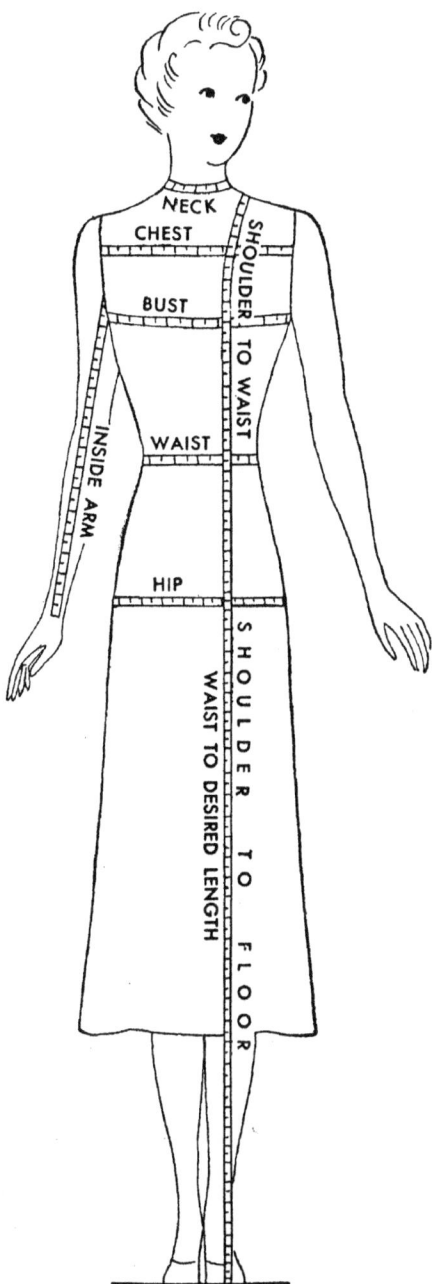

BUST (Fullest Part) . . . . ._____

WAIST . . . . ._____

HIP (Fullest Part) . . . . ._____

WIDTH OF CHEST . . . . ._____

FRONT WAIST LENGTH
Shoulder to Waist . . . . ._____

FRONT SKIRT LENGTH
Waist to Desired Length . . . . ._____

FRONT FULL LENGTH
Shoulder to Floor . . . . ._____

NECK (At Base) . . . . ._____

SHOULDER
Neck to Armhole Line . . . . ._____

ARMHOLE . . . . ._____

WIDTH OF BACK . . . . ._____

BACK LENGTH
Neck to Waist . . . . ._____

BACK LENGTH
Neck to Floor . . . . ._____

OUTSIDE ARM
Shoulder to Wrist (Arm Bent) . . . . ._____

INSIDE ARM
Armhole to Wrist (Arm Straight) . . ._____

UPPER ARM (Fullest Part) . . . . . . ._____

ELBOW (Arm Bent) . . . . ._____

WRIST . . . . ._____

HAND (Closed) . . . . ._____

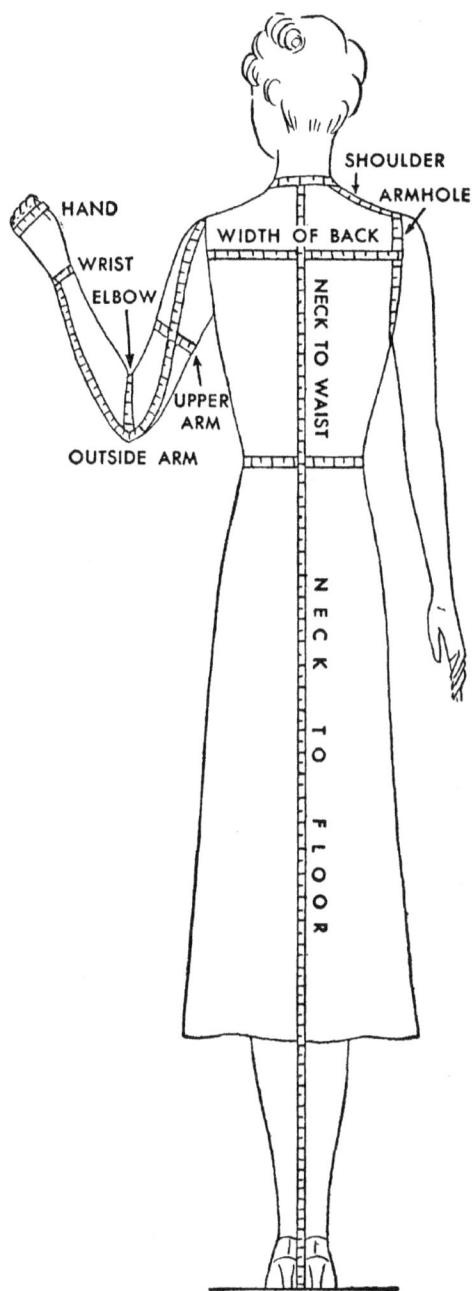

Keep Accurate Measurements

Since the garments in this book are all cut from measurements, it is necessary to have accurate ones to follow. Keep a list of your own measurements always at hand for ready reference.

Measurements for fitted garments should be taken over the type of foundation garments you expect to wear with them. Remove dress, jacket, or coat, which would distort the measurements. Do not take measurements too tight. Make all easy enough for comfort. The chart shows how to place the tape correctly for each measurement.

Making The Pattern

If you have the least doubt about your ability to chalk out the garment on your fabric, then rough it out first with crayon or heavy pencil on wrapping paper or newspaper. Cut out the paper pattern and use it to cut your garment. Cutting from a diagram, you can be sure that the proportions are correct for your size and that the garment will be a good fit.

THE SECRETS OF DISTINCTIVE DRESS

YOUR COLOR

A STUDY OF COLOR—THE COLOR FAMILY—COLOR NAMES
—DEVELOPMENT OF COLOR SENSE—COLOR CHARAC-
TERISTICS AND COMBINATIONS—SELECTING YOUR
COLOR—COLORS FOR VARIOUS TYPES.

I am going to talk to you about color—your color—in this chapter. A lesson in color is interesting and helpful. The very principles of distinctive dress embrace color, lines, and fabric, and one should never underestimate the important part they play in the matter of successful costuming.

Manufacturers and shopkeepers agree that a certain design may be very successful in a certain color and fabric but an absolute failure in another. Therefore, to use colors pleasingly and blend them harmoniously, one must understand them.

It is a recognized fact among salespeople that color is what first attracts a customer's attention, particularly in wearing apparel. The color of a gown or a suit is invariably decided before the kind or quality of fabric is considered.

Originally published in *The Secrets of Distinctive Dress, 1918*

Color expresses and signifies emotions, both physical and mental, a fact that may be verified by looking to nature, to the changes of color brought about by the changing seasons. Thus, the green of spring denotes freshness, youth, purity, and hope; the brilliant, glowing colors of summer are symbols of vigorous, ardent motherhood; the somber tones of autumn portray the richness and beauty of a successful maturity; and winter with its brown-gray trees, gray skies, and snowy whiteness, typifies the graciousness and tolerance of age.

Again color has been called the "music of light." The significance of this expression may be readily grasped by persons who have learned to see and to use color intelligently. Thus, the fundamental, or foundation, colors may be likened to the notes of a musical instrument—a piano, for instance. Both the variations and the harmonious combination of color are easily compared to the harmonies produced on the piano by a skilful, studied combination of the notes of a musical scale. Likewise, the light shades, the incidental or indefinite qualities of color, may be considered as would these same values in a musical composition, grouped to produce a pleasing sound or a pleasing spectacle.

You may study color in two general ways.

One way is by association—that is, by becoming so familiar with the various color combinations from actual observation as to be able to tell beforehand what the general effect will be. This knowledge is generally obtained by observing and associating with objects whose chief beauty lies in their coloring.

The other way is by studying the laws and principles governing harmonious combinations that have been formulated by persons who have made a special study of this subject.

By practicing the former method you may develop a fine sense of color; but without any theoretical knowledge the color combination will be limited to the copying of certain pleasing color effects that may be observed in art or in nature.

Once the laws and principles of color are clearly fixed in your mind, the combining of colors to bring out the best effects in dress can be done with confidence, and it is work that will grow more fascinating the more deeply you enter into it.

The practical application of the theory of color has not kept pace with many of the other branches of art and industry. This is not because its study has not been persistently and successfully followed by scientists, but because

"Therefore, to use colors pleasingly and blend them harmoniously, one must understand them."

those of their investigations which have been made available for the artizan are looked upon as being of doubtful value for practical purposes.

It is a common idea that the faculty of so combining colors as to produce artistic results is less a question of science than of a certain inborn taste, and that unless one possesses this peculiar gift it is of little use for him or her to attempt any color combinations.

That certain persons possess a decided taste for color, or, as it is commonly termed, "an eye for color," is beyond question. Parallel cases are found in the field of music, where certain individuals have a most pronounced gift for placing chords and memorizing melodies. But a lack of these particular talents in either field will not prevent you from gaining satisfactory results.

THE COLOR FAMILY

There are three primary colors: red, blue, and yellow.

Some noted artists in working with them said there should be seven colors, all the colors of the rainbow: purple (violet), indigo, blue, green, yellow, orange, and red.

A close study of Fig. 2 will show first the three primary colors; and then, by the combining of these three colors, how other colors, called secondary colors, are produced.

In Fig. 1, I am showing you a scale of colors with red, yellow, and blue—1, 3, and 5 —as a base and with the secondary colors, orange, green, and violet—2, 4, and 6. These colors may be further identified by R for red, O for orange, Y for yellow, G for green, B for blue, and V for violet.

To know color, you should first become thoroughly familiar with the three primary colors: red, yellow, and blue. Then you should learn how these may be combined to make the seven colors. Thus, red and yellow, two colors, make orange, a third color; yellow and blue, two colors, make green, a third color; blue and red make violet; and red, yellow, and blue make indigo, which is the only one of the combinations that is not considered as a secondary color.

Again, go back to Fig. 1. Think of the scale as cylindrical in form, as though you had it' cut out and were holding it up in your hand as a circle. You will see then clearly that the connecting hues between red and violet are omitted.

Consider red as your base. There are two kinds of red, red-yellow and red-blue. (The three red-blue colors, or shades, between red and violet are omitted from the scale through necessity of the black background. They are, however, red-red-violet, red-violet, red-violet-red, and should be considered in connection with the study of this scale.) Red-yellow is red in combination with a smaller quantity of yellow. Red-blue is red in combination with a smaller quantity of blue. The first color mentioned is the predominating color.

Next, consider yellow as your base. Yellow in combination with a small amount of red gives yellow-orange; in combination with a small amount of blue, yellow-green. Blue with a little red gives blue-violet; blue with a little yellow gives blue-green.

Study the color scale. Be sure that you understand first the three colors, then the seven. Then fix in your mind definitely that from these colors emanate all other colors.

Red extends two ways on the scale, into blue and into yellow. The colors extending to a point half way between red and blue and half way between red and yellow would come in the family of red, because they have red as a base. But to you, a woman, it would seem unfair to class all these beautiful shades and tints of red as red, although from a fine sense of color they are. You do not think of pink, flesh, orange, and even russet as red, yet they are of the same family, the same as blue-violet and blue-green are of the family of blue.

All the beautiful tones and hues of color should be appreciated.

It is very necessary in order to appreciate colors fully that you should know about color tones. Tones are developed by the addition of black for shades and white for tints.

It is necessary, too, that you should have a clear idea of hue, and this is shown in Fig. 1, which is really a scale of spectrum hues. If to a color is added a small amount of another color, a change in hue is produced. Thus, a little orange added to red gives red-red-orange, a hue of red. It is the hue of a color that often makes it becoming or unbecoming, a point that is well worth remembering.

When a color is suggested as becoming to you, make sure that you understand from what basic color it came. You might be able to wear, for instance, red-violet, which would be a soft plum color, but you may not have enough color and vivaciousness to wear blue-violet. You must see and realize that there are two distinct kinds of violet color, just as there are two kinds of blues, two greens, two yellows, two oranges, and two reds, and think of them in two colors, not just as blue, green, red, and violet.

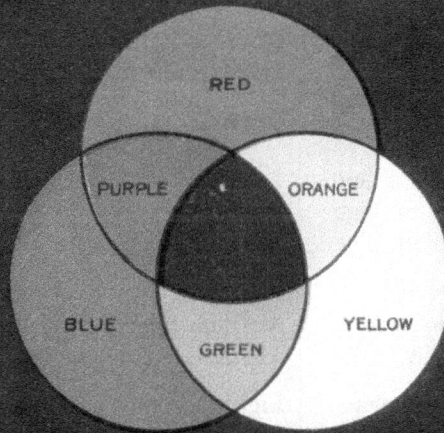

Fig. 2

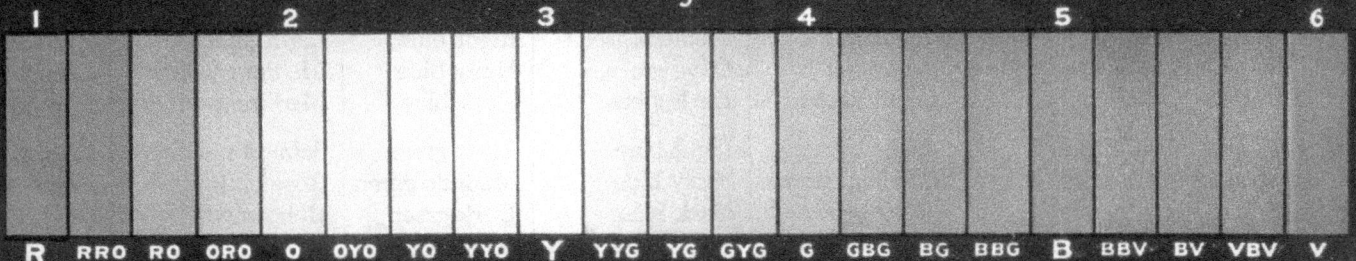

1			2				3				4				5			6
R	RRO	RO	ORO	O	OYO	YO	YYO	Y	YYG	YG	GYG	G	GBG	BG	BBG	B	BBV	BV	VBV	V

Fig. 1

68B § 2-113B § 1-206C § 18-I L T 67B § 1-102C § 18-126 § 2   COLOR CHART   A9-8 21

Principal Color		Perfect	Excellent	Strong	Good	Fair	Weak
Blue	Light	Cream	Light brown	Yellow	Olive green	Pink	Purple
	Medium	Cream	Medium brown	Yellow	Medium green	Medium red	Lavender
	Dark	Gold	Dark brown	Orange	Medium green	Medium red	Heliotrope
Brown	Light	Cream	Light blue	Myrtle green	Shell pink	Nile green	Purple
	Medium	Cream	Light blue	Medium green	Salmon pink	Reseda	Gray
	Dark	Gold	Turquoise blue	Medium orange	Rose pink	Medium red	Lavender
Drab	Light	Light blue	Salmon pink	Medium green	Red	Heliotrope	Cream
	Medium	Medium blue	Rose pink	Medium green	Wine	Lavender	Gray
	Dark	Dark blue	Rose pink	Dark green	Maroon	Purple	Yellow
Gray	Light	Light blue	Rose pink	Medium green	Red	Lavender	Cream
	Medium	Medium blue	Salmon pink	Medium green	Wine	Heliotrope	Tan
	Dark	Dark blue	Salmon pink	Dark green	Maroon	Purple	Brown
Green	Light	Light cream	Delicate pink	Purple	Wine	Medium gray	Light blue
	Medium	Medium cream	Rose pink	Yellow	Medium red	Navy blue	Light blue
	Dark	Medium gold	Rose pink	Orange	Dark red	Medium lavender	Light blue
Lavender	Light	Light purple	Delicate pink	Light brown	Medium gray	Light green	Yellow
	Medium	Light purple	Rose pink	Medium tan	Pale blue	Medium green	Red
	Dark	Dark purple	Ivory white	Dark brown	Light blue	Medium green	Maroon

Principal Color		Perfect	Excellent	Strong	Good	Fair	Weak
Maroon	Light	Cream	Light blue	Light yellow	Medium green	Medium tan	Scarlet
	Medium	Silver	Medium blue	Medium yellow	Medium green	Medium tan	Purple
	Dark	Gold	Medium blue	Medium orange	Dark green	Medium gray	Lavender
Orange	Light	Purple	Medium blue	Light green	Light brown	Gold	Yellow
	Medium	Purple	Medium blue	Medium green	Light brown	Gold	Cream
	Dark	Purple	Medium blue	Dark green	Medium red	Silver	Lavender
Pink	Light	Light blue	Lavender	Light tan	Light gray	Light green	Scarlet
	Medium	Medium blue	Heliotrope	Medium tan	Medium gray	Medium green	Red
	Dark	Medium blue	Purple	Medium brown	Medium gray	Medium green	Dark blue
Purple	Light	Lavender	Light green	Light yellow	Cream	Salmon pink	Red
	Medium	Heliotrope	Medium green	Medium yellow	Silver	Rose pink	Scarlet
	Dark	Lavender	Medium green	Orange	Gold	Medium gray	Scarlet
Red	Light	Cream	Light tan	Medium green	Light blue	Light yellow	Purple
	Medium	Silver	Light tan	Olive green	Navy blue	Medium yellow	Lavender
	Dark	Gold	Light brown	Dark green	Dark blue	Medium orange	Pink
Yellow	Light	Purple	Light brown	Light blue	Light green	Salmon pink	Cream
	Medium	Purple	Medium brown	Navy blue	Medium green	Rose pink	Silver
	Dark	Purple	Dark brown	Dark blue	Dark green	Heliotrope	Gray

NOTE.—In using this table as a reference to harmonious and distinctive dress, it is well to bear in mind fabric colors, tones, and shades as regulated by seasonal and style changes rather than artists' colors, so that a conception of correct combinations will result.

A woman whom I know well, whose eyes are brown and whose hair is red-brown, can wear any of the yellow or orange browns and can wear green-yellow perfectly, but blue-green gives her a lifeless, tired look, demonstrating that life in the color, when a definite color is used, is required for her particular type.

This same woman wears dark blue well, for the reason that there is no interference from the color of her frock, and her eyes, hair, and complexion dominate over the dark blue and supply that which the blue-green color tends to "kill."

In the table shown on pages 120 and 121, I have arranged a large number of color combinations that will serve to guide you in assembling colors. This table may be used freely, and while it does not cover all known colors you will find that it has sufficient combinations to simplify the selection of colors for dress.

COLOR NAMES

To obtain a good knowledge of the various color names that are applied to materials for dress, you will make no mistake in referring to the color cards issued from time to time by dealers in such materials, as well as by textile manufacturers and dyers.

So many of these cards have been issued and so many different names have been applied to colors that are alike that an attempt at standardizing the various colors has been made by various concerns that have united to form what is officially called The Textile Color Card Association of the United States, Incorporated.

This association has issued cards that should eventually prove valuable not only to manufacturers, but to dealers and individuals as well, for the colors are so numbered that it will be possible to match all materials and threads by number, provided the numbers assigned to colors by this association are adopted by all textile and allied industries.

To give you an idea of the manner in which this association has gone about this matter, I might state that a system of standard numbers has been established giving each color a number consisting of four figures that expresses as nearly as can be done the character of the color according to the following plan:

The first, second, and third figures indicate the relative proportions of the component parts of a color. Thus, the first figure indicates the principal color on which the shade is based, the second the principal blend, and the third the secondary blend. For the purpose of identification, white is numbered 1; red, 2; orange, 3; yellow, 4; green, 5; blue, 6; violet, 7; gray, 8; black, 9; and no change, 0. The fourth figure of the color number indicates the strength of the color designated by the first three figures. To the lightest is assigned the number 1; to the second lightest, 2; to light, 3; medium light, 4; medium, 5; medium dark, 6; dark, 7; second darkest, 8; and darkest, 9. In addition the abbreviation S., for standard, or O., for season number, is prefixed to the color number in order to avoid possible interference with established numbers.

To illustrate the system devised by this association, let us consider the color turquoise, to which is assigned the number S. 6153. As you will observe, 6 represents blue, the principal color; 1, white, the principal blend; 5, green, the secondary blend; and the last number, 3, the light strength.

Following is a list of the standard color numbers issued by this association, together with the name applied in each case:

1001	White	2007	Dark Cardinal
1041	Ivory	2009	Garnet
1045	Cream	2035	Geranium
2003	Scarlet	2063	Cherry
2005	Cardinal	2065	Ruby
2067	American Beauty	4285	Terra Cotta
2103	Pink 1	4287	Mahogany
2105	Pink 2	4383	Chamois
2107	Pink 3	4815	Gold
2131	Flesh	4817	Old Gold
2145	Salmon Pink	5005	Emerald
2163	Wild Rose	5007	Hunter
2165	Raspberry	5067	Myrtle

2167	Claret	5143	Nile Green
2169	Burgundy	5164	Ocean Green
2174	Ashes of Roses	5183	Mignonette
2183	Old Rose	5185	Reseda
2185	Strawberry	5385	Bronze
3005	Orange	5413	Chartreuse
3025	Burnt Orange	5485	Olive
3083	Tan	5495	Evergreen
3115	Maize	5823	Sage
3183	Écru	5827	Bottle Green
3185	Fawn	6005	National
3187	Beaver	6007	Yale Blue
3285	Gold Brown	6053	Saxe Blue
3295	Brown	6055	Electric
3485	Topaz	6057	Sapphire
3842	Buff	6083	Marine
3925	Chestnut	6085	Navy
3928	Seal	6103	Light Blue 1
3945	Tobacco	6105	Light Blue 2
3948	Negro	6107	Light Blue 3
4005	Lemon	6109	Light Blue 4
4025	Golden Rod	6123	Cornflower
4115	Leghorn	6153	Turquoise
4123	Apricot	6183	Copenhagen
4183	Champagne	6185	Delft
4185	Beige	6505	Peacock
6853	Cadet	7205	Fuchsia
6855	Regimental	7285	Magenta
6925	Navy 2	7814	Heliotrope
6875	Navy 3	7817	Prune
6985	Midnight	7905	Egg Plant
7003	Violet	8065	Steel
7005	Pansy	8067	Slate
7007	Purple	8111	Pearl Gray
7123	Lavender	8113	Silver
7163	Lilac	8115	Nickel
7183	Orchid	8843	Castor
7195	Amethyst	8845	Taupe
7187	Plum	8935	Smoke
7195	Wisteria	8965	Graphite

DEVELOPMENT OF COLOR SENSE

With the principles of color understood, you may readily turn to the application of color in dress, so that appropriate color schemes for given purposes may be developed. The ways in which to become familiar with color combinations are numerous.

Once you have become sufficiently experienced to define hues, tints, and shades, and have trained your eye to observe and your memory to retain normal colors with their variations, you will be able to learn much from nature's combinations, be it in cloud and atmospheric effects, autumn tint and foliage, flowers, minerals, animals, birds, insects, and so on.

Then, by visiting museums and exhibitions, you may study effects in china, glass, and textiles, including tapestries, rugs, and old embroideries and laces; or by frequenting the art galleries, you may gain inspiration from old and new Japanese prints and from the exhibits of old and new masters in art.

Again, the ballroom, automobile shows, and other places where variety and gaiety in dress may be seen will help to give you ideas of color, to say nothing of the theater and even the motion-picture playhouses, where old-period gowns and other equally interesting styles and colorings are often portrayed.

You may also get inspiration from the beautiful colors in the shops and show windows. Indeed, many a beautiful gown has been created by designers who, having seen some beautiful creation, were inspired to apply their knowledge of color, line, and fabric.

Taste in color is largely a matter of civilization and cultivation. The nearer a person approaches the savage, the greater is the inclination for brilliant colors; yet it is true that many excellent effects are attained by savage races. As civilization advances, the reverse is true, the colors being less severe and leaning more to the soft, quiet tones, in imitation of nature.

Nature has given to each of us a keynote of color. It is helpful to study and fully appreciate her judicious and well-proportioned uses, and it is interesting to know that she uses but comparatively small quantities in proportion to her range of the intense or bright colors. Her greens, grays, and browns are enlivened by but small touches of blue, red orange, and other bright colors.

It is always best, as far as possible, to preserve Nature's proportions when following her suggestions. Once, when asked regarding appropriate dress by a ponderous woman who was dressed in red velvet, a prominent lecturer on dress harmony made this reply: "Madam, Nature made some butterflies and some humming birds red, but she made elephants taupe, and Nature, madam, serves as a good color criterion." This answer is a wise though somewhat curt illustration, emphasizing the fact that brilliant colors must be used in small quantity, and shades in bulk.

Some of the color combinations most frequently met with in nature are the white and yellow of the daisy; the brown and yellow of the sunflower; the yellow and purple of the pansy; the light salmon, yellowish green, cream, and moss-green of the tea rose, which affords an ideal suggestion for a combination of delicate tints; the American beauty rose, with its hues from violet to red, together with the tones of green in the leaves. The nasturtium, with its tones of yellow and orange and its tender green foliage, is a fine example of combining warm colors. A bunch of grapes, with its various catawba shades, or shaded from green to blue and violet, is also full of suggestions. Then there are the browns, pinks, greens, rose pinks, reds, and grays of the autumn leaves as a source of inspiration. So the list might be extended indefinitely by exercising the faculty of observation.

COLOR CHARACTERISTICS AND COMBINATIONS

To become familiar with the colors used in dress, look into their characteristics.

Blue may be regarded as a standard color for woman's dress. It not only gives the impression of coolness, but is restful and unobtrusive. The lighter tints are very closely related to white, and when it is the purpose to make white give the impression of purity a bluish tint is always given to it. On the other hand, when mixed with black, blue produces a black that gives the impression of greater blackness. Blue frequently is preferred to black, because it is not inclined to look grayish in combination with some of the other colors.

Every season brings its new range of colors. Many new colors—some queer, some positively ugly—are presented as being the very latest and, of course, the most fashionable colors. The various exploiters of fashion proclaim each color as desirable, but invariably, after all is said, the assertion is made that blue is good and will be worn, thus emphasizing the power of popular demand.

Blue is always fashionable, because women instinctively understand its value as a garment color, and it predominates because it best enhances the good points of the wearer, in both the figure and the complexion. It does not by its intensity or depth obliterate the real charm of the face or form; neither does it accentuate any unpleasing features.

White in its different varieties, the same as blue, may be called a standard, because it, too, is universally becoming, but the same thing cannot be said of black. Black is not becoming to nor desirable for all women, as it emphasizes age and adds as many years to a face as white will subtract from it. A prominent writer credits the French women with saying that black should not be worn after a woman is thirty, unless for mourning, nor again until after she is sixty, and then only if she feels that she has to wear it.

Violet is more pliable in its combinations than some of the other colors. It associates well with green-yellow, yellow-green, orange, orange-yellow, yellow, gold, gray, and green, but rarely is it satisfactory with red or blue, unless some intermediate tone or a neutral color is used with it.

The darkest shades of orange form pleasing combinations with subdued yellows, especially when a stripe or a small figure of black is worked into the material. Light orange is too bright to be used freely, but yellow-orange or gold can be used to good advantage for embellishments.

Green is very restful to the eye and forms an agreeable harmony with white. Its effect is to lend brilliancy. Light greens upon dark grounds produce pleasing effects, while the reverse is less satisfactory. Light and grayish greens are desirable in plain materials or as stripes, figures, or borders of darker tone. Blue-green, however, is difficult to combine with other colors, combining best with gold and with red in small quantities.

When you combine colors, you must be careful not to injure the purity of one by an excess of another. For instance, light blue and light pink go well together, because neither is sufficiently intense to overpower the other. But an equal quantity of light blue and normal red will not harmonize, because the greater intensity of the red will overpower the blue and make it look sickly or faded.

Thus, it will be seen that when the intensity of colors differs greatly, the quantity of each that is used must also differ in order to produce a combination that is harmonious; that is, the intense color must be used in much smaller quantity as·a trimming or outline to the lighter one in a given color scheme.

As I have stated before, colors that contrast harshly may be blended into harmony by placing intermediate hues, tones; or the neutrals between them. Thus, black, white, or gray between strong, bright colors neutralize them and prevent confliction. Very bright colors in quantity are detrimental to somber ones when placed side by side.

SELECTING YOUR COLOR

If you select the right colors for your dress, everybody concerned derives satisfaction from your intelligent choice.

Most persons experience real pleasure or displeasure from colors, some claiming that certain colors affect them to the extent that they cause happiness or depression, according to the way in which the individual views them.

It is claimed, too, that right color in one's dress has a beneficial effect on the health of the body and the mind of both the wearer and the observer. Indeed, it cannot be disputed that different colors produce different effects on the individual—that they excite different and varying states of feeling. This undoubtedly accounts for the pleasure and comfort so often experienced in wearing some particular garment.

A regrettable thing, however, is that we can seldom define this feeling or credit it to the proper cause; it is unfortunate, too, that the effect of color on different persons is as widely different as the effect of musical sound, for just as there are persons devoid of sound appreciation, that is, with no ear for music, so there are persons without a color sense, a defect that is usually designated as color blindness or color ignorance.

The lack of this faculty, fortunately, is less frequently found in women than in men, and this may be attributed to the fact that with the advance of civilization men have practically discarded color in its broad uses, whereas women have clung to color, not only for their dress, but for their home decoration.

One of the natural and God-given duties of woman is to charm and please, and color

Goldwyn Pictures   *Photo by Mishkin*

MAE MARSH

Wearing an exquisite bouquet, showing that she truly appreciates the
virtue of happily adapting harmonious color in herself

rightly used is a wonderful factor in accomplishing this end.

If I were asked to give a color standard for woman's dress that could be adhered to continuously, I would have to confess that it is practically impossible. Each season produces new shades, tints, or tones of colors that cannot be classified, and these may put at variance any method that might be worked out during a previous season.

Of course, if the advice of advocates of a standard type of dress for women were followed, it might be possible to plan garments for them in much the same manner as men's garments are planned. While much may be said for and against the adoption of such a standard type of dress, its discussion here is not warranted; yet I must emphasize that such a style would have a tendency to take away from woman the privilege she has of bringing out her best points. As matters now stand, there is much unattractive color in woman's dress; yet how much more displeasing, yes, even distressing, might be the effect if we could wear no colors save the somber blacks, blues, browns, and grays that constitute the color range of men's clothes.

Color is and should be made to express personality.

Often it is made to do this only crudely, even offensively; and too often it serves to express but the foolish desire to attract attention or to be attired in what is considered the latest fashion.

Color should charm and delight the observer and fit in most harmoniously with surroundings; it should be an expression of one's best thoughts.

Love of color is not to be condemned, for color should be made the means of enhancing real beauty of face and form and an aid in clarifying and idealizing plain features of face and figure. Too often it is allowed to lessen the effect of real beauty and to accentuate ugliness or plainness of feature.

In selecting color for yourself, you must always make sure of whether or not it suits your individuality. Do not rush headlong after the newest color on the counter simply because it is new, although in this respect I feel safe in saying that a sufficient number of colors are brought out each season to suit all types and to meet all demands.

Personal coloring depends on health and happiness, as well as on sickness and sadness, so that a shade or a tint that is becoming to you at one time may be found very trying at another. Besides, you should take into consideration the color and texture of your skin, and the color of your eyes and hair. Particularly should you follow this advice if Nature is beginning to dim the color and brilliancy of your eyes and to turn the natural color of your hair to gray or white. Under such circumstances a readjustment of color is advisable. The tint or the shade must be varied; that is, lighter or darker tones should, almost invariably, be resorted to.

Brilliant, hard, cold colors, or what might be fittingly termed unrelenting or non-retiring colors, should be avoided once a woman is past her first youth; in fact, not every young woman or young girl can afford to wear such tones. For instance, pure blue, red, or yellow, grass green, the popular golf red, and similar colors that are launched forth nearly every season as being the latest thing are so strong that they rob the wearer of all the natural color of skin, hair, and eyes, making even a young, vigorous girl appear devoid of animation and charm.

The use of such colors even as trimming is a mistake commonly made by women lacking in the natural color of skin, hair, and eyes, such women unquestionably believing that because of their own lack of color it is the correct thing to use colors of this kind.

You will do well to note that gray eyes reflect blue or green, and sometimes brown tints, and that the right shade of blue will increase the color and brilliancy of blue eyes.

Blue face veils give the effect of having clarified the skin and heightened the color, and are for this reason a pleasing accessory to many women's toilets. Face veils of white, however, should be avoided except by the very youthful and those having a clear, highly colored complexion.

It is important that you consider your eyes, hair, and skin in choosing colors for your dress, being careful to avoid those which will give you a faded, unhealthy tinge, or too harsh and florid an appearance, and choosing that which will enhance the beauty of your individual coloring.

Your attention is called to the surprising changes that are brought about in a person's appearance by light showing through colored fabrics, especially those used in gaily colored parasols. A green parasol makes red hair appear brown; violet eyes, bluish-green brown; red lips, brown; white skin, green; black gloves, greenish-brown; and a green coat, deeper green. An orange parasol makes a snow-white forehead appear orange colored; rosy cheeks, scarlet; red lips, scarlet; the neck

and skin where the reflected light strikes, orange; yellow gloves, yellow-orange; and a black coat, maroon.

The lining in coats should have consideration. Many women like beautiful linings, and in the linings of their coats indulge this fancy to their hearts' content. But great caution should be exercised in selecting a coat lining, so that when it is thrown back in a theater, in a hotel dining room, or in any place where it will be seen, the lining will make a suitable background for you and your gown. Many times the color of the lining may be such that it will be very effective and add much to the "picture," but if it is a jarring color, the effect may be entirely spoiled.

You may be interested to know, too, that color in dress materials is affected by light, all colors being lessened or increased in richness, brilliancy, or beauty according to whether they are seen in daylight or under artificial light. Therefore, in selecting colors for evening garments, you will profit by examining the materials under artificial light and those for day wear in daylight.

In selecting silent-tone fabrics, you will likewise do well to avoid the influence that other colors or more brilliant hues exert. For instance, if you desire a very dark blue, take the material where other colors will not detract from it, and in this way its real tone and color will assert itself. Very often a soft, beautiful color will be killed by being placed close to a color that is more brilliant.

Still another factor that you should reckon with in the selection of color is its seasonal adaptability. Shakespeare's advice to actors to "suit the action to the word" might well be paraphrased in advice to women to "suit the color to the season."

Climate and season are closely related to the color and weight of garments, and they demand considerable thought if one is to be appropriately and artistically dressed.

It is indeed distressing to see a woman dressed in red, warm brown, yellow, or orange on a warm day in June or July. Although beautifully glowing in winter weather, such colors are shunned by the tasteful dresser in warm weather. Instead, she will wear gowns and hats of white and light tints, of blue and its related colors, green and violet, and other cool colors, so as not to produce a sense of warmth or heat.

Nature, as I have already remarked, serves as an excellent guide in color selection, and she may always be followed to advantage in matters of dress.

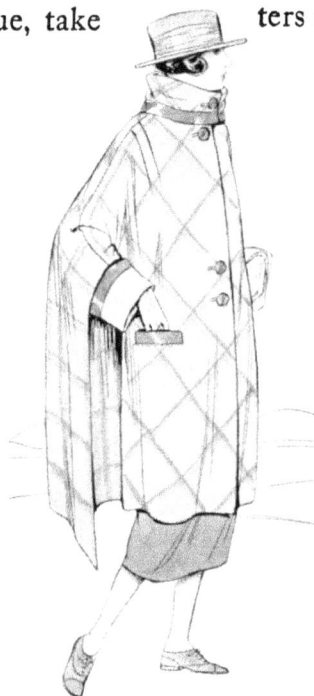

In the spring, Old Mother Nature does not consult the fashion books, but puts forth the beautiful violets, primroses, hyacinths, and daffodils. In her scheme of coloring she harmonizes the fresh green of the trees with the pink petals of the apple blossoms and the delicate coloring of the springtime flowers. Her color scheme is so near perfection that no one has been clever enough to improve on it. In summer, she modifies these colors, making them less brilliant, thereby creating an atmosphere of coolness and comfort; in autumn she turns the foliage to the soft browns, tans, and russets, suggesting appropriate colors for this season; and as snowy, bleak, cold winter steals upon us, she warns us to defy the icy blasts by dressing warmly and putting on bright colors suggestive of heat and warmth.

Black and cold gray, which display no cheerfulness, are colors given over to sorrow, calmness, and the passing out of this world. They are not appropriate for the joy manifested at the dawn of spring, when everything in Nature's garden thrills with happiness. White, however, is always symbolic of purity and repose, is ever dear to us, and is most often worn in summer.

By following Nature, that is, giving correct thought to appropriateness in the matter of color and choosing gowns and wraps suitable for each season, there will be little chance for repetition of color in your wardrobe; likewise, there will be greater opportunity for you to work out a color scheme in gowns, wraps, hats, shoes, and accessories and thereby avoid the extravagances in dress so often accredited to women.

COLORS FOR VARIOUS TYPES

To aid you in the selection of color, I have introduced here a table that shows which colors may be worn successfully, as well as which colors should be avoided, by the eight recognized types of women: the fair blonde; the Titian, or red-haired, blonde; the blonde-brunette, or "in-between" type; the pale brunette; the olive brunette; the florid brunette; the sallow mature woman; and the fair-skinned mature woman.

In using this table you should keep in mind that a woman's age must always receive due consideration. Deep pink, for example, is usually for the youthful, while for the woman of sixty or more, white, delicate pink, flesh, rose, mulberry, black, dark blue, gray-blue, gray, and some shades of purple, such as lavender and pink-violet, are the most becoming.

COLORS THAT MAY AND MAY NOT BE WORN BY DIFFERENT TYPES OF WOMEN

Type of Woman	Black	White	Brown	Blue	Green	Gray	Purple	Red	Yellow	Pink
Fair Blonde Hair—flaxen or golden. Eyes—blue, gray, or brown. Complexion—clear; little color.	Good; especially if of high luster and with touches of bright colors and white.	Good; especially clear or oyster white.	Good; especially very dark shades and green-brown, or bronze.	Good; all shades, if not too brilliant, including delft, turquoise, and peacock.	Good; both light and dark.	Good; especially pearl, dove, and warm shades.	Good; especially heliotrope, wisteria, and blue-violet.	Dark and brilliant shades, like golf red, are best.	Avoid all except very pale yellow.	Good; all delicate or subdued shades, from lightest to old rose.
Titian Blonde Hair—red. Eyes—blue, gray, or brown. Complexion—medium clear and clear white; varying color.	Good; especially transparent black.	Good; especially cream and ivory.	Rich, deep, dark brown is all right. Avoid tans and yellow browns.	Good; especially blue-gray, midnight or darkest navy, and soft, silent tones.	Use only darkest shade of pure color and bronze. Avoid light green unless complexion is very clear and color good.	Good; especially gray with a pink cast.	Avoid. If complexion is clear and white, darkest and lightest lavender or violet may be used.	Avoid.	Fair. Dark, rich orange or amber tones are best as trimming, or veiled by white or black.	Lightest tints all right. Shell and flesh best.
Blonde-Brunette, or "In-Between" Type Hair—light chestnut or brown tone. Eyes—hazel, gray, blue-gray, or brown. Complexion—medium.	Fair; good if used with trimmings of color or white.	Good; especially clear white or with pink tint.	Fair; pinkish tan and golden brown best.	Good; intensifies the color of blue-gray eyes. Avoid very bright hues.	Fair; especially blue-green.	Clear or blue-gray fair. Avoid combinations of gray and black.	Fair; darkest shades are best. Very clear complexions may wear lavender.	Good in darkest shades, especially if used with very dark blue.	Palest yellow fair. Avoid écru tints.	Good; especially pale pink and rose.
Pale Brunette Hair—black or dark brown. Eyes—brown, gray, or blue. Complexion—clear. Skin—fair; varying color.	Good, if white vest or collar is used or if delicate color of soft material is used as trimming.	Good; especially pure cream and ivory.	Fair; all shades.	Good; all shades. Electric and sapphire excellent if eyes are blue.	Only some shades of bronze, reseda, and bottle are good.	Good; all shades, especially pearl, dove, blue-gray, and color gray.	Fair; must be used carefully. Orchid is good.	Only dark red, such as garnet and burgundy, is good.	Mustard, amber, and canary yellows are best.	Good; all pinks, except where cheeks are highly colored.
Olive Brunette Hair—dark brown or black. Eyes—clear brown or black. Complexion—dark in tone. Skin—smooth. Lips—very deep red, sometimes with a purplish tinge.	Avoid.	Excellent; especially ivory and cream.	Fair in very dark shades. Mahogany with cream for collar is excellent.	Excellent if very dark.	Good in dark, silent tones.	Fair if warm color gray.	Use cautiously. Egg plant is permissible.	Excellent; especially the dark, warm shades.	Terra-cotta or fawn shades are good if cautiously used. Apricot in sheer material or as trimming is excellent.	Excellent in delicate tints. Salmon is especially good.
Florid Brunette Hair—black or dark brown. Eyes—black, brown, or gray. Complexion—dark. Skin—highly colored.	Very good; especially with color touches and yokes of cream or écru lace.	Good; especially cream and ivory.	Good; especially golden, tan, and nut browns.	Very pale, dark, or peacock, devoid of purple tinge, is best.	Dark green is best.	Silver gray is best.	Avoid. Not becoming.	Cardinal, crimson, and clear red are best.	Good; including any tone from orange to ivory.	Coral, rose (pale), old rose, and flesh are best.
Sallow Mature Woman Hair—gray or white. Eyes—brown, blue, or gray. Complexion—sallow, without color.	Good only with white or cream and touch of bright color.	Only cream and milk white are good.	Avoid.	Midnight navy, without any tinge of purple, are good.	Avoid.	Good when of warm color gray.	Avoid, except in dull tones and with white at neck. Some lilac may be used.	Avoid, except in dull wine shades and with white at neck.	Avoid.	Only old rose is good.
Fair-Skinned Mature Woman Hair—gray or white. Eyes—blue, brown, or gray. Complexion—fair; good coloring in lips and cheeks.	All right if relieved by white or palest écru collar, yoke, or vest.	Excellent.	Very dark, but not golden, brown is good; seal and chestnut are best.	Use only dull old blues, pastel tints, and midnight blue.	Dark shades treated the same as black are good.	Stone and lighter tones relieved by white at neck and brightened by a touch of color are all right.	Use only heliotrope (dull tone), grape, and darkest shade.	Avoid.	Use palest buff only.	Use palest and wild-rose shades only.

From youth to old age, every woman can wear white. Of course, not all women can wear pure, or blue, white, but then there are the milk, cream, and pink whites from which to select.

Also, it is well to know that all cold colors should be avoided by persons with sallow complexions; they should resort to warm colors and tones. A person with a perfectly clear complexion, though, may wear any color that does not clash with the color of her hair.

The range of colors given in this table for the Titian, or red-haired, blonde may with slight variations of shades and tints be safely followed in all the varying degrees of complexion.

Black for the pale-brunette type is always less trying if a cream-white vest or collar is used with it, or if some delicate color in soft material is employed as trimming. Brown is not good if the complexion is imperfect or inclined to noticeable sallowness or if the eyes lack the brilliancy characteristic of this type.

The sallow mature woman is by far the most difficult type of woman to dress. For this reason, great care should be exercised in the selection of every color given for this type in the table. Any color selected should be of the gray, shell, or pastel tone, rather than of brilliant quality. Bright colors introduced to give character or develop design should be used intelligently and very sparingly. Large splashes of color should never be used near the face, because this will not have the desired effect of brightening up the face, as is usually supposed, but will add to the sallowness of the complexion. Even white should be of the soft milk, cream, or pink tint, rather than a pure, or blue, white, which is as hard and brilliant as if it possessed color.

The part of the table for the fair-skinned mature woman contains information for the prematurely gray-haired woman—that is, the woman whose hair is the only indication of approaching age and whose coloring and figure still retain their youthful qualities—and also for the mature woman who cannot be robbed of the brilliancy and beauty of complexion or youthful figure by age.

The prematurely gray may successfully wear materials of mixed color, such as two-tone fabrics in which the less vivid color predominates; that is, fabrics in which the more brilliant color is the underwoven color. This type can wear rather brilliant colors also, provided they are veiled with transparent white, black, or dark colors of somber tone.

To broaden your knowledge of color, think not only of the colors for yourself, but also of colors appropriate for your friends. This will increase your interest in color as well as in art, for color is a requisite of art, and a knowledge of art comes by study and application—comes to you only through conscious effort.

Artcraft Pictures Photo by Victor Georg

ELSIE FERGUSON

Who knows clothes and how to make them carry the lines of dress to
success for her as she herself carries the lines of the play

Vintage Notions Monthly continues to share the work of Mary Brooks Picken and the Woman's Institute which inspired my book *Vintage Notions*. Although the Institute was founded 100 years ago, the treasure trove of lessons and stories are still relevant today and offer a blueprint for living a contented life.

If you enjoyed this issue of *Vintage Notions Monthly*, visit AmyBarickman.com for more of my curated collection of vintage content including patterns and books for needle and thread, inspiring fabric and textiles & free vintage art every Friday. Be sure to tune in to *Vintage Notions* episodes for a guided tour through my collection of sewing and fashion history, as well as modern projects inspired by my extensive library.

Vintage Notions Monthly, Issue 16 (VN0204)

For wholesale ordering information contact Amy Barickman, LLC at 913.341.5559 or amyb@amybarickman.com, P.O. Box 30238, Kansas City, MO 64112